I0155425

Threads

WEAVING DISCIPLE MAKING INTO THE FABRIC OF YOUR LIFE

KIRK FREEMAN

CROSS**BRIDGE**
BOOKS
SAN ANTONIO, TEXAS

Threads: Weaving disciple making into the fabric of your life. Copyright @2023 Kirk Freeman

Available online at DiscipleMakingThreads.com

Threads / Kirk Freeman
ISBN: 979-8-218-31113-1
Library of Congress Control Number: 2023921102
Christian Books & Bibles / Christian Living / Spiritual Growth

Edited by Caroline Winston
Cover design: Camryn Richmond
Author photo: Breeanne Leonard
Interior design: Mandy Pallock

This book is typeset in Charter and Avenir Next.

Printed in the United States of America.

CrossBridge Books, an outreach of
CrossBridge Community Church
PO Box 592569
San Antonio, TX 78259-2569
DiscipleMakingThreads.com

Rev. 06-2025

Kirk Freeman is one of the most gifted and passionate disciplers I know. This book will change your paradigm of discipleship and give you tools to put it into practice. By the time you're done, you will enjoy your relationship with Jesus even more.
　　—Mark Batterson, New York Times bestselling author of *The Circle Maker* and Lead Pastor of National Community Church

The best disciple-making training is reproducible and transferable. It can be done by anyone, anywhere. Kirk has clearly done this in his own life and ministry and Threads captures this essence. This book is so helpful and simple. I plan to recommend it to everyone I coach and mentor.
　　—Jeff Vanderstelt, Executive Director of Saturate, founder of Soma, and author of *Saturate, Gospel Fluency, Making Space,* and *One-Eighty*

Kirk Freeman has been a dear friend over three decades and I've had a front row seat of seeing his message of discipleship lived out and reproduced, impacting the world around us.

Threads is a breakthrough book for us who are committed to being disciples who make disciples, a rare treasure hidden in a field and my encouragement to you is that as you read this, you, too, will impact the world by being a disciple who makes disciples.

So grateful for Kirk Freeman and his family for the life they live and model in discipleship, as disciples of Jesus who disciple their family, church body, and leaders in their city. Kirk has given us a discipleship framework that works. So many times, discipleship is a platitude or a desire but not fully lived out. Kirk guides us in *Threads* to do the same as we all seek to make disciples everywhere we go.
　　—Jimmy Seibert, Founder and Senior Pastor of Antioch Community Church and Senior Leader of the Antioch Movement

I consistently encourage seminary students to view their studies as an act of Christian devotion and discipleship. This volume reveals the wisdom of perceiving and approaching the whole of the Christian life in terms of being and making disciples. In so doing, Threads reminds us afresh of Jesus' charge to every generation of Christians to follow him and to make disciples for him. Here, Kirk Freeman demystifies discipleship and disciple-making, even as he prioritizes it for any and all Christ-followers. A needed corrective and timely resource for churches and ministers!

—**Todd D. Still**, PhD, Charles J. and Eleanor McLerran DeLancey Dean & William M. Hinson Professor of Christian Scriptures, Baylor University, Truett Seminary, Waco, TX

Discipleship was never intended to be a class, but a series of conversations that create room for the Holy Spirit to create transformation that leads to multiplication. Thus, what we celebrate other will imitate. *Threads* is not just another book on the allusive subject of disciple making. This is a field guide for an adventure into the depths of human relationships yielding an unquenchable joy in Jesus. My friend, brother, and colleague has not just written a masterpiece, he is by definition this book! *Threads* is pastor Kirk Freeman! I've been renewed and refreshed personally by this ministry of discipleship from this resource and so will you.

—**Dr. Ed Newton**, Lead Pastor, Community Bible Church, San Antonio, TX

For Kirk Freeman, faithful discipleship cannot simply be limited to small groups studying the Bible, praying together, and learning essential content. Rather than viewing discipleship as a subject to be mastered, Kirk grounds his unique approach in the deeply relational, intimate, biblical metaphor of the bride and the bridegroom. *Threads* takes us inside the heart of a pastor, who shares, with remarkable (and often entertaining) transparency, his own missteps and misperceptions in learning to follow the command of Jesus to "make disciples of all nations."

—**Mark DeVries**, pastor, author, and founder of Ministry Architects and co-founder of Ministry Incubators

I have known Kirk for over 14 years as pastor and friend and the wisdom in *Threads* that he offers has been ploughed and practiced, fought for and refined. In a world of ministry with great theories but sometimes little fruit, I have had the privilege of watching these truths in Threads change the trajectory for individuals, families and ultimately a church and beyond at CrossBridge. The fruit can be observed and I have seen it. These chapters contain wisdom that is easily digestible for an often sought after plan for discipleship. Jesus didn't intend for it to be hard and draining, but life giving. Kirk offers practical guidance so that everyone can step in to a life of being "Jesus centered, with a Kingdom calling, with footprints designed for others to follow." His passion for "letting the bride encounter the groom" has turned his church into a flourishing family who looks like they should – joyfully on mission and with eyes on God. I am grateful for him and these pages – every church should look with new eyes at the concept of discipleship and glean from his years of planting and harvest.

—**Jen Barnett**, Executive Director, Freedom Prayer

Threads is a reproducible and accessible model of Discipleship that we use with great effectiveness in our community. You will be amazed what Jesus will show you and how eager others are to practice enjoying Him.

—**Jeff Harris**, Gracepoint Church, San Antonio, TX

Threads is an encouraging account of Jesus Christ renewing Kirk Freeman's heart for ministry with the reminder that following Jesus requires making disciples who make disciples. Freeman expertly magnifies the Scriptural fibers of discipleship to encourage a renewed imagination of disciple making woven throughout church life.

—**Chris Johnson**, Senior Pastor, First Baptist Church San Antonio, TX

CONTENTS

PART II: FOR PASTORS AND LEADERS

APPENDIX

Acknowledgments

No one ever says "thank you," unless they've received something. I'm definitely a man who has received something, so I'm saying thank you to CrossBridge Community Church for being the oven in which this cake was baked and for sticking with me for over 20 years as I've learned to be a pastor. Also to the staff team that makes "going to work" way more fun and inspiring than I ever imagined it could be. I'm grateful to Shawn Sullivan who kept praying that Jesus would awaken my heart to disciple making (he did!), and to Brian Hannas for all the conversations about how we make disciples who make disciples.

I'm thankful to the over 200 pastors who walked through some version of this disciple making training over the years and who share a commitment with me to become disciple making churches.

I'm blessed to have a family of daughters and sons-in-law who are just as committed to disciple making as I am, which means I can almost always find someone off of whom I can bounce ideas.

Thanks also to Mandy Pallock who used her talents and joy to guide me through the publishing process from start to finish. (She'll gladly do the same for you: Productions@Pallock.com).

And...I'm eager to say thank you to my best friend and wife, Debbie, who lived through the slow evolution of this book. She listened as I processed it out loud and was my chief encourager.

Foreword

One of the hardest things for a pastor to overcome is the obsession with numerical growth. Don't get me wrong, growth is not only good but essential. In my estimation, if something isn't growing, it's in the process of dying.

As one studies the book of Acts and the rise of the church, we see a total of seven progress reports that each state how rapidly the church was growing (Acts 2:47, 6:7, 9:31, 12:24, 16:5, 19:20, 28:30-31).

Peering into the gatherings of the very first church that assembled in living rooms across Jerusalem we immediately see that they didn't grow because they were focused on growing. Rather, they grew because they were focused on their devotion to the apostle's teaching, to fellowship, to the breaking of bread, and to prayer (Acts 2:42) They were committed to developing their relationship with Christ as their first priority. From this starting point, they were being transformed day by day from the inside out as individuals and more importantly, as a community.

This internal spiritual combustion compelled the first believers to meet the needs of the people around them expecting nothing in return. They were simply paying forward what they were receiving from their personal relationship with Christ. As you might suspect, they gained the favor of the neighbors around them who in turn were eager to belong to this loving community of Jesus followers.

The paragraph ends with this statement: "And the Lord added to their number daily those who were being saved."

In a nutshell, the first church grew not by focusing on numerical growth but spiritual growth of the members. The focus wasn't first on evangelism but on discipleship. As the new believers were being discipled, authentic outreach and evangelism followed organically.

God is saying, you take care of the disciple making, and I will take care of the growth. Hard for the modern pastor to do, but it's the right strategy. I believe the people in the "pews" are longing for it.

This is not only something that my good and longtime friend Kirk Freeman believes in, but he has also put before us an effective plan to get us there. He presents a practice that has been born out of the church he has pastored for the last **twenty** years. It has been proven.

What Kirk is offering is intentionally anchored in Scripture. But what Kirk lays out goes way beyond good content. It is more of an experience that awakens people to the joy of being in a relationship with Christ. The Core Experiences embedded into the disciple making process are eloquent and life-giving. They point us in the right direction which results in a modality of flourishing. The secret sauce of what Kirk presents us—that has already helped hundreds of churches—is revealed in the title: *Threads*.

In the pages before you, he is going to challenge the church to not see discipleship as a single program but as an opportunity to *weave* discipleship into every aspect of the life of the church and family. Truthfully, this is the only approach that will prove to be efficacious over the long haul.

As I read this wonderful work, I found myself becoming quite hopeful. What if followers of Jesus and whole churches took what Kirk is offering seriously and got after it? Well, I think what we saw in the first century just might happen again in the twenty-first century. Amen…so be it!

RANDY FRAZEE
Pastor and Author

THE BEAUTY OF WEAVING

Every summer of my childhood my family would spend part of our summer vacation in Red River, New Mexico in the mountains on the edge of the Wheeler Peak Wilderness Area. Hiking and picnics were our main activities, but sometimes on rare occasions, we would make the 45-minute drive through the desert on Hwy 150 to Taos.

Taos is now the vacation spot of the wealthy, but it wasn't like that back when I was a child. At any rate, it wasn't the small city that intrigued me most as a child, but rather what was on the outskirts of Taos, a pueblo that was and is one of the longest continually inhabited settlements in North America. People native to America still live there and claim over 1,000 years of tradition.

I only recall snatches of memories from my first visit there as a 7-year-old. The adobe home, the ovens cooking bread, the dancers wearing the vibrant colors of their traditional clothing. And of course, the gift shop where my parents bought me a little drum (a purchase they regretted for the rest of our vacation…until it was lost…or was it?… Come on, Mom, fess up.)

The most enduring of the memories I have was of the time we entered an adobe home and found a woman weaving a blanket on a loom. Threads of colors of the brightest hues were being crisscrossed. Patiently, persistently, her hands retracing motions learned from childhood, the weaver would navigate the horizontal thread across vertical threads—over some, below others— each adding a small layer. Each an expression of the image seen only in the weaver's mind, each one becoming an inextricable part of the intricate fabric.

In Part I of *Threads,* I'll share a way of disciple-making that is biblical, life-giving, and reproducible. It's *all* about learning to genuinely enjoy and follow Jesus in a way that we can show others. It's all about relationship. It's a way of disciple making that can be woven like threads into every aspect of your life and your church.

A big part of this is what I call the Core Experiences. These biblical experiences are fundamental to all human relationships and families. In fact, in the context of human relationships, we all acknowledge their importance. For some reason, though, we don't often apply them to our relationship with Jesus, and as a consequence, we often don't fully enjoy Jesus. Because of this, disciple making becomes a content-focused exercise that is more about transferring information than an actual relationship. As a result, disciple making might not be very life-giving or reproducible.

On the other hand, when we start with Scripture and weave these Core Experiences into the fabric of our lives, we begin to relate to Jesus as if he were actually real—which he is!

What's more, we simultaneously become equipped to share this life-giving relationship with others. No matter where we are or who we are with, we have everything we need to be included by Jesus as he reveals his great love and lordship to others. All of life becomes an opportunity! Approaching disciple making this way has been more fun and fruitful than anything I've done before.

In Part II, I'll speak more directly to pastors and leaders—those responsible for leading in the church setting.

I remember the excitement I felt when I first began seeing Jesus come alive to the people I was discipling using the Core Experiences. As the pastors and leaders of our church began doing the same thing, they too shared stories of how their disciple making groups were more fruitful.

At that point, our team confronted what now seems like the most obvious of questions:

WHAT IF DISCIPLE MAKING WERE A THREAD WOVEN THROUGH EVERY CONTEXT OF THE CHURCH?

What if the Sunday morning gatherings, the children's ministry, the parenting ministry, the student ministry, the home groups, the D-groups (discipleship groups), and even our staff meetings all had disciple making as their goal?

WHAT MIGHT HAPPEN IF EVERYTHING WE DID BECAME DISCIPLE MAKING?

In Part II, I'll describe the journey a growing number of churches are on to do exactly that. Instead of relegating discipleship to a course, a ministry department, or even a small group of men or women meeting for Bible study, these churches are intentionally leveraging every ministry context for its disciple making potential.

To realign the church in this way requires a cultural change which takes time and persistence, but the fruit along the way will keep you motivated and committed. It works! And it works because it's aligned both with the fundamental elements of relationships and with Jesus' strategy in the Great Commission.

If you choose to start your own journey, here's what I think you'll discover:

- If you're a disciple maker, you'll find a way of discipling that is more life-giving and less driven by content and structure.
- You'll find people you disciple actually enjoying Jesus and eager to follow him in making disciples.
- If you're a pastor, you'll discover a ministry approach in which the yoke is easy and the burden is light just like Jesus said it could be.[1]
- If you're a parent, you'll find practical and powerful ways to weave disciple making into your family in a way that helps your children experience the very real presence of Jesus.

The best way to make a disciple is to disciple them. It's actually a bit hard to write a book about the principles of experiencing and enjoying Jesus—it's much easier to show it than tell it. For that reason, at the end of Threads, you'll find an invitation to experience these principles with me in a short-term cohort. I'm not an expert, but I am unswervingly committed and willing to share.

For now, though, let's get to weaving...

---

1 Matthew 11:30

CHAPTER 1

LEO AND THE LORD

"WHEN PEOPLE EXPERIENCE JESUS, EVERYTHING CHANGES."

Leo was staring at me like my dog stares at a bug he's never confronted before. If you've got a dog, I'm sure you know the look I'm talking about…it's when they cock their head at an angle to one side and then back to the opposite side at the same angle as they try to process what this new bug is. If you could read their thought bubble, it would say, *You are so strange. I don't have any idea what you are.*

That's how Leo was looking at me, only Leo wasn't a dog. Leo was a young man in his 20s, wearing a backpack and walking through San Pedro Park in downtown San Antonio.

A few other pastors and I had gone to a park to pray for our city when Leo saw us. I had just finished praying and opened my eyes to see Leo giving me the angled-head, dog stare. As the event concluded, I stepped off stage and walked over to Leo. After I had introduced myself, we had a casual conversation about what our group was doing which easily led to a spiritual conversation. I asked him a simple question that my friend Shawn Sullivan had taught me:

IF GOD COULD DO A MIRACLE IN YOUR LIFE, WHAT WOULD IT BE AND COULD I PRAY FOR YOU?

It's always amazing to me how simple things can be so profound and reproducible. The "Miracle Question" is one of those. Leo responded to my question by sharing that he was in recovery and about to start Narcotics Anonymous (NA). The miracle he hoped for: *I want to be clean.*

I asked Leo if I could pray for him right then and with a shrug of his shoulders, he replied, "Yeah sure, sounds good." I briefly asked the Lord for his power and peace to come upon Leo and to bring about the cleanness he was seeking.

When I finished, I told Leo that there had been a time in my life when I'd lived with a constant feeling of not being good enough. While this was different than Leo's struggle with substance abuse, I had definitely been unable to shake my tendency to think of myself in this negative way. As a result, I was easily angered and struggled with insecurity. This went on for years until someone showed me that through following Jesus and trusting in his love and forgiveness, God would view me as acceptable— as good enough! When I first heard this, I somehow immediately knew it was true and instantly felt the chains of failure and inadequacy fall away.

It only took me about 15 seconds to share that story with Leo, and when I finished, I asked him, "Have you ever experienced something like that?" He said he hadn't but that he'd been thinking that maybe God was something he needed to start looking into. I immediately thought that God was serving up the perfect opportunity for me to share the Gospel, but Leo quickly said he was supposed to meet someone and needed to leave.

Before he left, I gave him a little booklet I keep in my wallet that explains the good news of Jesus and how to put your trust in him. I told Leo that the information in this booklet had changed my life and that I really would like him to read it tonight before he went to bed. He promised that he would, and I showed him that I'd written my name and number on the back should he want to talk more. That was it. Nothing more happened—at least that I could see.

Six weeks later though, to my utter surprise, I received a voicemail from…that's right, Leo. Here's what he said, "I just started NA and we're supposed to pick a higher power. I read that booklet you gave me and chose Jesus as my higher power, but I don't know what to do now."

I have to admit, I was shocked! I share gospel booklets with lots of folks, but I rarely have someone call me back six weeks later. I was blown away and couldn't wait to see what God was doing. I quickly called Leo back. He basically repeated what he'd said in the voicemail, "I've chosen Jesus as my higher power, but don't know what to do now." I suggested we get together to read the Bible because it talks a lot about Jesus. In the laid-back way that I later realized was characteristic of Leo, he said, "Yeah sure, sounds good." (Hang with me, the story is only going to get better.)

When Leo and I tried to schedule a time to connect, we realized we lived on opposite sides of the city, about 45 minutes apart. Since the pandemic taught everyone how to Zoom, I suggested we try that, and Leo said (all together now), "Yeah sure, sounds good."

Leo didn't own a Bible, so in our first time together, I helped him download the Bible app, and we used a simple method called a Discovery Bible Study (DBS) to read and discuss the story of Zacchaeus. To give you a sense of Leo's spiritual background, his family was Catholic, but he'd never had a Bible nor had he heard of Zacchaeus. (Note to self: Pick a Scripture with names that are easier to pronounce.)

In a DBS, after reading the passage a couple of times, participants discuss a couple of basic questions:

1. What does this passage show you that's true about God, his nature, his priorities, etc.
2. What does this passage show you that's true about people, their nature, priorities, etc.

Anyone can jump in and participate in a DBS, regardless of background or spiritual context, and Leo was all in with our conversation. Without knowing anything previously about Jesus, Leo shared some powerful truths about him from what he read:

"Jesus notices people."

"Jesus knows people's names."

"Jesus isn't as judgmental as people."

"Jesus takes time for people."

Our conversation (or Bible study) lasted all of 15 minutes, after which I told Leo something else that was true about God: He loves to speak to those who are willing to listen.

I asked Leo if he'd like to try to listen to the Lord. He replied...you know what he replied: "Sure, sounds good." He grabbed a pen and sheet of paper and I asked him to write this on the card:

"LEO, I WANT YOU TO KNOW..."

After we'd both done this with our respective names, I told Leo that I was going to pray, asking Jesus if he would speak to us, and then we were going to be quiet and wait for about one minute. We were going to let Jesus complete the sentence for us, and we were going to write down whatever came to our minds.

Let me press pause on the story for a moment. At this point, I don't think Leo was yet a follower of Jesus. Using church-talk, Leo wasn't yet "saved." He certainly had no biblical knowledge beyond what he'd just read about Zacchaeus. He didn't know much about the cross, nothing about the resurrection, and I'm sure he'd never heard of the sinner's prayer.

Interestingly though, most of the folks in the first century who gathered to hear Jesus were pretty unaware also. Jesus spoke to those people back then, and I figured he would speak to Leo, too. And I wasn't wrong...now back to the story.

After one minute, I asked Leo what he'd heard and how he'd finished the sentence. This is what he read to me:

Leo, I want you to know that I'm really glad that you want to know more about me. I've been wanting this for a long time. If you'll keep reading the Bible, you'll get to know me more.

Jesus said to Leo pretty much the same thing he told the crowds in biblical times, "Come to me. Follow me." Honestly, this is what he's saying to everybody who doesn't yet know him.

After Leo had read to me what he'd heard, he looked up wide-eyed and asked, "Is that really Jesus talking?" Rather than sharing with Leo the deep well of wisdom I'd acquired over the years (please roll your eyes here), I pointed him straight back to the Luke 19 narrative we'd just read.

I asked Leo, "Does what you heard sound anything like what Jesus said to Zacchaeus?" Leo looked again at his Bible app for a second, then looked back at me with a big smile and said, "Yeah! What Jesus said to me is like what he said to Zacchaeus—I guess I *did* hear Jesus—cool!"

Leo had just listened to the Lord and the Lord had spoken to him in a way that was:

- Consistent with Scripture
- Consistent with God's character
- Positive and not condemning

It was my joy to tell Leo that his experience wasn't rare—Jesus loves to speak to those who will stop to listen genuinely. I then told him that when Jesus speaks, he generally wants a response from us,[2] so I asked Leo to write down what I call an "I will…" statement to express what he will do this week in response to what Jesus had said.

Leo took all of about 10 seconds to write his "I will…" statement and then, with the look of a man who had found a treasure map, he shared with me his commitment: "I will read my Bible every day this week."

Leo who was still battling drugs, had almost no meaningful spiritual background, and had never studied the Bible in his life or much less thought of Jesus' speaking to him had just made a commitment to read his Bible every day (and to listen to the Lord, I might add).

That day if we'd just talked about Zacchaeus without listening to the Lord, do you think Leo would've made an unsolicited commitment to read his Bible every day? If I'd told Leo that his "homework" was to read the Bible every day, do you think he'd have done it? Not on your life. But when Jesus spoke to him—well that's a different thing altogether.

When people experience Jesus, everything changes.

When people experience Jesus, everything changes. When you get to be included in it, that day becomes the best day of your week!

---

2 John 14:23 Jesus replied, "Anyone who loves me will obey my teaching. My Father will love them, and we will come to them and make our home with them."

CHAPTER 2

THE WEDDING

"IN A WEDDING, THE ONLY THING THAT TRULY COUNTS IS THAT THE BRIDE MAKES IT ALL THE WAY TO THE GROOM."

Never had I spent so much money and yet had so little control. It was my daughter's wedding. For years my wife and I had anticipated this day—both in our prayers for our daughter's future husband but also in our effort to put aside a little money every month for the day we would celebrate and consecrate their union. Now, after 25 years, it was actually here.

I have to admit, I'm most comfortable when I'm in charge. Lots of folks are like that. But in the hierarchy of wedding planning, I wasn't even on the org chart. Despite having been responsible for generating most of the finances that made the food, venue, dress, invitations, hair stylist (and about a hundred other things) possible, it was understood that in this venture, I was a silent partner. My wife Debbie and my daughter were driving the bus; I was along for the ride. Initially, I had resisted this minority role, but after taking part in a discussion about color palettes and

15 different shades of pink, I became forever grateful to not be included in the minutia of wedding planning. Just tell me when to put on the tux, and I'll be there.

Finally, the moment for putting on the tux had arrived. My daughter and I were standing on the outside of the adobe chapel in the hill country of Texas, facing two beautiful, hand-carved wooden doors, eagerly anticipating the crescendo in the music when the doors would be opened and, with all eyes glued on her, she would begin her journey down the aisle to her groom. When the moment arrived and the doors opened, I counted three seconds (one Mississippi, two Mississippi...) and together she and I began walking—slowly and elegantly as I'd been instructed—down the aisle. Smiles and photos met us on both sides and as we made our way, I stole a glance at my daughter. Subconsciously, I think I expected her to look back at me, sharing the excitement of the moment with me, but I couldn't have been more wrong. She never looked at me once. Her eyes were fixed on her groom. Beaming and beautiful, step by step, as if magnetically and irresistibly drawn, she went to him.

In a wedding, the only thing that truly counts is that the bride makes it all the way to the groom.

It was in this instant that I realized that nothing else mattered. All the planning, all the tastings, all the tours of venues, and everything else that goes into preparing for a wedding in our culture—none of it matters if, when the big wooden doors swing open, the bride doesn't make it all the way down the aisle to the groom. In reality, if the bride doesn't make it to the groom, all you have is an incredibly expensive catastrophe (and a whole lot of little sandwiches with the crust cut off). In a wedding, it's not about the bride's relationship with any of the guests, or even with the special person leading her toward her beloved. In a wedding, the only thing that truly counts is that the bride makes it all the way to the groom.

So it is with disciple making. This is what John the Baptist meant when he told his followers in John 3:29-30: "The bride belongs to the bridegroom. The friend who attends the bridegroom waits and listens for him, and is full of joy when he hears the bridegroom's voice. That joy is mine, and it is now complete. He must become greater; I must become less."

CHAPTER 3

A DEFINITION OF DISCIPLE MAKING

"TO ENJOY AND TO FOLLOW JESUS TOGETHER IN A WAY THAT WE CAN SHARE WITH OTHERS."

There was a time in my life when I used the term "disciple making" or "discipleship" in a very limited way. It primarily referred to a group of 3-4 men or women studying the Bible together, praying for one another, and holding one another accountable in various ways. Additionally, I might have used discipleship to refer to any number of spiritually-themed topical classes.

I still think of those contexts as disciple making, but now I use the term more broadly to describe:

- The whole mission of my life.
- The whole mission of parenting.
- The whole mission of the local church and all of its ministries.

As to a specific definition of disciple making, our team would say:

> Disciple making is learning to enjoy and follow Jesus together in a way that we can show others how to enjoy and follow him too.[3]

We use this language because it carries the aroma of relationship—the fragrance of a wedding. My own marriage to my wife, Debbie, has grown in parallel with this definition in important ways. For over 30 years now we've enjoyed learning to live life together while learning to follow Jesus together, and we've done both in the presence of our three daughters, each of whose ideas about marriage (on our good days and our bad days) were formed by our example. Disciple making is about enjoying and following Jesus together because marriage is about these things. The joy and the connection Jesus desires to share with his bride (the church) can only come when the bride actually experiences her groom in life-giving relationship.

Disciple making does, of course, involve studying and learning, going and doing, but not at its root. The root is always "enjoying and following Jesus." I think this may have been what Jesus meant when he exhorted us to abide in him in John 15.

In Jim Wilder's and Michel Hendrick's important book, *The Other Half of Church,* they share how God designed our brains to process reality utilizing two hemispheres and how this design impacts our spiritual growth. One of their most illuminating assertions is this:

---

3 It's not imperative that you adopt my definition of disciple making. What is vitally important is that your definition emphasizes the personal nature of the relationship Jesus offers and the important of obedience.

Left-brained discipleship emphasizes beliefs, doctrine, willpower, and strategies but neglects right-brain loving attachments, joy, emotional development, and identity.[4]

So much of disciple making in the Western world emphasizes the left brain but neglects the right brain. The liability in this approach is that God designed our brains so that we process our reality first and fastest through our right brain, as Wilder and Hendricks say:

…we often know things faster than we are conscious of them and definitely faster than we can speak about them.[5]

While the brain is much more complex than this short description, I bet you're already seeing the application for disciple making. I'm also guessing that most of your disciple making experience has prioritized information, doctrine, and behavioral change rooted in willpower. This is a more left-brain approach.

Imagine what disciple making might look like if we included the left brain and the right brain, or as Wilder and Hendricks say, "The whole brain." What if instead of focusing on telling, we focused on *showing* and *experiencing?* What if disciple making began with actually learning to enjoy Jesus—to feel his presence, to hear his spiritual voice, to know his comfort?

This is actually the biblical model reflected in almost all of Paul's epistles. The following are just a few of the ways he emphasizes the importance of experiencing and attaching ourselves to Jesus:

---

4 Wilder, J., and Hendricks, W., (2020). *The Other Half of Church.* Chicago: Moody Publishers, 25.
5 Ibid. 21.

EPHESIANS 1:17

I keep asking that the God of our Lord Jesus Christ, the glorious Father, may give you the Spirit of wisdom and revelation, so that you may know him better.

EPHESIANS 1:18-19

I pray that the eyes of your heart may be enlightened in order that you may know the hope to which he has called you, the riches of his glorious inheritance in his holy people, and his incomparably great power for us who believe.

COLOSSIANS 1:9

I pray that God might fill you with the knowledge of his will through all the wisdom and understanding that the Holy Spirit gives.

When we miss this, we always wind up somewhere Jesus never intended for us to be. Sometimes we fall into religiosity, striving to do good or learn more. Even though we believe at one level that we're saved by grace, at another level we're doing our best to prove our worth. We can become condescending and judgmental toward others and even harder on ourselves.

This is one of the reasons why enjoying Jesus is a good filter through which to view our lives. Be honest and ask yourself this question: Do I enjoy Jesus? Do I feel close to him, like being with him, have fun with him? Is it uncommon for you to think, *"Jesus really likes me!"* It shouldn't be, because he actually does.

A NEW IDENTITY

When a groom and a bride come together at a wedding, the bride walks out with a new name. As evidence of their oneness, the groom shares his name with his bride. She literally has a new identity (with a new driver's license to prove it).

Jesus has given us a new identity. Previously we were enemies of God—that was actually our name. Our minds were set on rebellion against him as evidenced by our sinful actions and decisions.[6] Now in Christ we have a new identity: we are dearly loved children, holy, faultless, and blameless.[7] Together we were enemies of God and now we're called the Bride of Christ. Talk about a change of identity!

Jesus uses the two most intimate human relationships to describe how he feels about us and the kind of relationship he desires to share with us. It's amazing!

There is not a loving relationship we have that doesn't stir our emotions and feelings.

While feelings don't trump faith, there is not a loving relationship we have that doesn't stir our emotions and feelings. In a marriage, spouses should feel cherished most of the time. If they do not, something is wrong. In the same way, children should feel confident in their parents' love.

Being a disciple is all about learning to live in this new identity, enjoying and following Jesus. Disciple making happens when we help others learn to enjoy and follow him too.

Because our new identity is the precious gift of Jesus, our spiritual enemy will use any and every means to obscure this precious, powerful reality. If the enemy can undermine the truth of our God-given identity in our minds, we will relate to Jesus as a criminal to a police officer, or

6 Colossians 1:21
7 Colossians 1:22

a student to her coursework, or a salesperson to their boss, or a million other distorted ways, but we won't enjoy Jesus. If we don't enjoy him, we won't follow him.

When experiencing Jesus becomes a central part of disciple making, the groomsman (the disciple maker) creates an aisle (an opportunity) for the bride (the disciple) to experience the groom (Jesus). When this happens, Jesus himself affirms the new name and new identity that he has given them.

HEADING INTO THE PRACTICAL STUFF

I'm about to describe for you what our team believes to be the Three Values of a disciple maker.

I'll follow this by describing Core Experiences with Jesus that serve as the foundation for a relationship of enjoying and following him.

Last, I'll share with you how we weave these Values and Experiences into every aspect of our lives and of our church.

In this book, you may find fewer concrete steps or methods than you expected. I'll share some, but not a lot. The reason is that methods always change—the Values and Experiences won't. If you internalize the Values and Experiences, you'll discover creative and effective ways to weave them like threads into your own life and into the fabric of your church.

CHAPTER 4

THREE VALUES OF A DISCIPLE MAKING CULTURE

"METHODS WILL BY NECESSITY CHANGE OVER TIME. VALUES NEVER DO."

"Ugh, that was miserable." That's what I told Debbie one night as we were leaving our Lifegroup. (You might think of this as a home group, cell group, house church, etc.) Debbie and I love these people, and they love us, but honestly, lately our Lifegroup had begun to feel more like a Deathgroup.

Something was definitely missing. The regular people were regularly coming, which previously was a metric I'd used for success, but the problem was deeper and more serious than that. Here's some of what I was seeing:

- The depth of vulnerability was low.
- If Debbie and I had to miss, the Lifegroup usually abandoned our normal practices and defaulted to a "fellowship" night of just eating/talking. (Not a bad thing, but it was every time I missed Lifegroup.)
- While people were nice to a guest who somehow found their

way to our group, no one was actively seeking to invite or share our Lifegroup with others. (Maybe they thought it was a Deathgroup too!)

- Raising up new leaders was difficult.
- Multiplying the Lifegroup was nearly impossible.

I could continue this list, but I'm betting you can already relate. I was distressed. I'm the lead pastor of the church, and the Lifegroup I'm leading is becoming a Deathgroup—yikes, not a great situation! What made things worse was that I'd been training folks for eight years in our church to lead Lifegroups. I cringed to think what the experience was in those other groups! *Lord, help me! No, literally, Jesus, you seriously have to help me!*

In response to my genuine cry for help, the Holy Spirit faithfully revealed the answer for turning Deathgroups back into Lifegroups. More than that, he showed us that the very same answer would transform our disciple making efforts in our men's and women's discipleship groups (as well as in our Sunday morning gatherings, and in our children's and student ministries.) The answer wasn't to adopt a new format or methodology. Instead, it was to adopt the biblical values essentials to making disciples who make disciples.

Our team needed to re-examine our values. Through more meetings and discussions than I like to recall, we released our existing values and embraced three more fundamental ones that had a profound impact on everything we did. We found that almost every problem we faced was rooted in our neglect of these three. We found that every solution we needed was also tied to these three values.

VALUE 1: WE ARE JESUS-CENTERED

Imagine this scene: you're a guest at a wedding, everyone has taken their seats, the groom is standing up front flanked by the wedding party of beautiful bridesmaids (with beautiful bouquets) and handsome groomsmen (each standing with their right hand over their left). The flowers, the colors, the lighting, and the music are all perfect. Then, at just the right moment, the big doors hiding the bride swing open, and the mother of the bride stands, followed by all in attendance. The bride, with eyes locked on her misty-eyed groom, is making her way down the aisle when to everyone's utter shock, one of the groomsmen leaves the groom's side, jumps into the middle of the aisle, and begins enthusiastically telling the bride all about the wonderful attributes of the groom. Instead of helping to create and guard the aisle, as one of the groom's trusted companions, this groomsman positions himself between the bride and groom, in a completely unnecessary effort to convince the bride that she should come to the groom. That groomsman in the aisle…that was me.

That groomsman in the aisle…that was me.

In no wedding in any era or any culture does the groom need assistance in drawing the bride to himself. With an unobstructed view of her groom, she will make her way to him every time. Our bridegroom, Jesus, certainly doesn't need my help. He is infinitely more captivating than I. The bride needs only to catch a clear glimpse of him—if I would just get out of the way. While this is so obvious, there was a disconnect in my mind when it came to ministry and disciple making.

For example, in our Lifegroup, I talked more than anyone, Debbie and I hosted most of the time, I played the guitar during our worship, and when we were in our "Bible discussion" time it was hard for me to resist sharing my wisdom and being the dominant voice. (This isn't just a problem lead pastors have, by the way.) The Lifegroup was me-centered rather than Jesus-centered. No wonder it felt like a Deathgroup sometimes.

Jesus is the Way, the Truth, and the Life—not me!

I experienced the same problem in my D-group (discipleship group) of three to four men. Often, much of our time was devoted to my explaining something. I might have been elaborating on Scripture, explaining a deeper layer of theological implication, correcting a misconception, or just sharing some bit of wisdom I'd gleaned from walking with Jesus far longer than the guys I was discipling. What's tricky about this is that generally speaking, nothing I was telling the guys was wrong. It was all correct, good, and even wise. Not only that, but I enjoyed doing it, and the other guys usually appreciated the insight I shared. No harm, no foul, right? Except...I kept getting in the way of our experiencing Jesus.

Let's be honest: there is no way our human words of wisdom or experience can adequately describe or touch the deep place of another person's heart the way that Jesus can and in the way that Jesus desires. He loves to include us in this process, but ultimately the bride needs only a glimpse of the groom to be drawn by the promise of love in the gaze of his eyes.

What if our disciple making objective became to let the bride encounter the Groom?

What if that became our objective in every disciple making context: to let the bride encounter the Groom. Oh, how much easier ministry, disciple making, and even parenting would be if our aim was to give those we disciple (especially our children) a glimpse of Jesus!

Almost every Christian already believes this is possible. That's why we so commonly say that God is inviting people into "a personal relationship with Jesus Christ." We know that the hope to which

Jesus has called us is an intimate, deep, forever, personal relationship with him…and yet, so often it seems that we treat Jesus completely impersonally. We treat him like a subject to be mastered. We focus on covering content, as if information acquisition were synonymous with intimacy. It simply is not.

In Scripture, God describes the relationship he desires with us in terms of a groom/bride and, elsewhere, a parent/child. In doing so, he's giving us a frame of reference for understanding what we can expect from him and what he expects from us. Because these are the two most important of human relationships, every person on the planet probably knows more about what God wants of them than they initially think they do. Even while we are unmarried we know that faithfulness, fidelity, vulnerability, intimacy, enjoyment, and commitment are part of a healthy marriage. Even if our relationship with our human parents was horrible, we know inherently that protection, love, provision, hope, correction, encouragement, and gentleness are all attributes of a good parent.

In Jesus-centered disciple making, the discipler takes their place to the side of the aisle so the bride can see the groom.

Why do you think that is? Why do you think that we all know these things and more about these two types of relationships even if we don't have personal experience with them in the human realm? The answer is simple: We were each made to experience this kind of personal relationship with God. He hard-wired us for a relationship with him—a personal, intimate, gentle relationship with him.

When disciple making is Jesus-centered, we give the other person (again, particularly our children) the opportunity to actually experience this kind of personal relationship with God through the Word of God and the Spirit of God. Regardless of the actual disciple making method, when it is Jesus-centered, we take our rightful place in the wedding party to the *side* of the groom where we get to see him do what only he can do—captivate his bride. When he does, everything changes.

This principle is so important that one of our three core values is:

We are Jesus-centered.

VALUE 2: WE HAVE A KINGDOM CALLING

One of the most frustrating and dismal ways to live this life is to live for what I call the six "P's" of this world:

1. Pleasure
2. Power
3. Popularity
4. Profit
5. Possessions
6. Pain avoidance

To be sure, most people are living this way and the state of the world reveals the futility of it.

By contrast, Jesus is calling us to live for his Kingdom — a calling much higher and much greater than the six "P's" the world chases. Jesus wants to include us in what he's doing in the world. "Come with me!" was his call to Peter, to Leo, and it remains his call to every one on the planet. As we say "Yes!" to him, we get to join him in expanding his Kingdom where we encounter the abundant life he promises.

We often refer to efforts aimed at inviting people into Jesus' kingdom as "evangelism" and we commonly use the term "discipleship" to express our efforts to expand the kingdom inside each other. While I'm not kicking those terms to the curb, they don't seem to capture the amazing reality they're intended to describe: Jesus wants to include us in everything he does—everything!

Jesus wants to include us in everything he does–everything!

Return again to God's wedding metaphor... the marriage proposal traditionally issued by the groom is an invitation to share his entire life—for richer or poorer, for better or worse—with his cherished bride. When a man drops to a knee, professes his love to a woman, and presents her with a diamond, he is *proposing* that they do all of the rest of their lives together—so is Jesus. His death and resurrection represent the O.G. of marriage proposals.[8] All human marriage proposals are reflections of his wonderful, exhilarating offer to include us in everything he does—forever!

For too long I treated what's commonly referred to as discipleship and evangelism as consecutive seasons of maturity. This was my default setting: *Discipleship was learning more about God. After you knew enough information or facts about God, you could advance to evangelism where you confronted other people with that information.*

Those last two sentences sound like the least exciting kind of life I can think of. Jesus died and rose for us to have a personal relationship with him, which means he wants us to live life with him! He's not sending us off to boarding school to learn about him, awarding us a certificate of completion, and then deploying us as a recruiter to send others to the same boarding school. He wants us to learn about him, to

---

8 For those over 40, O.G. is an abbreviation for Original Gangsta which is slang for the first and original version of a particular thing.

enjoy following him, and to grow deeper in love with him by including us in everything he does!

God is so excited about including us that he uses another metaphor to describe the fun and significance in which he wants to include us. He calls us ambassadors. Think about a person who might be appointed as an international ambassador nowadays. They're usually highly competent, they love the culture to which they've been sent, and they are usually good and trusted friends of the president who selects them. When a person is invited to be an ambassador, the president is saying essentially, "Out of all the people I know, I trust you to represent me to these people." That's what Jesus is saying to you! You're his trusted friend, his confidant, and the one he has chosen to represent his love to others, especially those in your oikos.[9]

One of the best ways to enjoy Jesus is to join him in what he's doing in the world.

This is the Kingdom calling Jesus gives to each of his followers. One of the most outrageous lies of our spiritual enemy is that this Kingdom calling is a "have to" kind of thing. It's not—it's a "get to" kind of thing.

People have always desired to share their favorite things with those they love. We get that from Jesus. He wants to share with us the things he is most excited about, and what's at the top of that list? More people coming face to face with his love for them.

My biggest disciple making errors have occurred in not connecting people with their Kingdom calling soon enough. In an oversimplified kind of way, one might divide disciple making into two segments: growing

---

9 *Oikos* is a Greek word used in the New Testament for "household." Households at that time generally included a broader group of people than they do today. I use oikos to refer to a person's sphere of influence: the people with whom they live, work, and with whom they interact regularly.

inwardly and going outwardly. My mistake was discipling people in these segments consecutively rather than concurrently. Rather than bringing them into the Kingdom calling on day one, I would focus on them going deeper inwardly until they reached a point where I felt they "knew enough" to go outwardly, taking the good news of Jesus to their oikos and beyond. The very real weakness of this approach was that I was never good at discerning when a person had reached the point of knowing enough. In fact, they almost never knew enough, and so disciple making seemed like a never-ending quest for growing deeper inwardly.

Years ago, after consistently discipling a couple of men weekly, I realized to my chagrin that they were no closer to becoming disciple makers themselves than they were when we had begun meeting together twelve months prior. To make matters worse, the thought of becoming a disciple maker had probably never even crossed their minds. Whose fault do you think that was? (To quote Scooby Doo: "Ruh-roh!")[10]

Once again, the wedding metaphor really has helped me here. Put on those "wedding goggles" and look at my old way of disciple making through the lens of the personal relationship between a groom and bride. Imagine a groom telling his bride, "In six months, after I've seen you mature as a bride and you know more about marriage, I plan on sharing something with you that's really important to me." Or what if a groom were to say, "I compartmentalize my life and don't want to share certain parts with you right now." That, my friends, would be C-R-A-Z-Y. (Guys, this isn't a marriage book, but you can consider that free advice. Don't do it.)

I didn't intend to disciple this way, but it's almost inevitable unless the disciple understands the big picture up front: You have a Kingdom calling because Jesus wants to include you in everything he's doing in the world!

This is one of the key reasons why my Lifegroup had felt like a Deathgroup—I wasn't connecting people to some of the most exciting experiences Jesus had for them.

---

10 Hanna-Barbera. Saturday morning cartoons. 1976 (even footnotes can be funny.)

With the central value of Kingdom Calling established, evangelism ceases to be merely one spiritual theme among many. Instead, through the Kingdom calling, a disciple is introduced literally to a whole other world of experiencing Jesus that is fulfilling, motivating, and worth talking about. This principle is so fundamental to a disciple making culture that it found its place as the second of our core values:

We have a Kingdom calling.

VALUE 3: WE LEAVE FOOTPRINTS FOR OTHERS TO FOLLOW

Sometimes when I would meet with guys for a D-group time, I didn't have a plan. If I did, it was this: We'll pick a passage of Scripture, discuss it, and then, at some point I'll slide into "teaching" mode and the guys in the group will slide into "listening/sleeping" mode until we run out of time and have to close in prayer and rush off to work. Sounds life-giving, right? (Yawn). I'm exaggerating a bit, but not entirely. Other times, I used a prepared Bible study from a book or some other source. While this may sound like the perfect solution, it's still a bit like having a groomsman in the aisle between the bride and Jesus.

If I want to raise up disciples who actually can and will go and make disciples of others, then I have to do everything in a reproducible way. I define reproducible like this: Doing everything in a way that someone with different or even lesser giftedness could do it themselves.

> **Reproducible disciple making: Doing everything in a way that someone with different or lesser giftedness could also do it.**

Before I understood this, I discipled intuitively, relying on my years of experience with Jesus, my previous knowledge of the Bible, and whatever teaching gifting I possessed. Generally speaking, most folks I discipled would say they grew spiritually during this disciple making season, but they seldom, if ever, were able to disciple others. I wasn't leaving any footprints behind for them to follow. I hadn't shown them or trained them how to do with others what I had done with them.

The problem? Intuition isn't reproducible. Intuition isn't scalable—it doesn't leave footprints for others to follow. I'll be the first to admit, discipling by intuition has an appeal to it—most people I discipled this way enjoyed it. In effect, they were content with learning from the groomsman who jumped into the aisle. Sadly, many Christians are content because it's all they know. We settle for watching, listening, and following a groomsman or bridesmaid who personally experiences the Groom, but we stop short

Intuition isn't reproducible.

of experiencing the fullness of what Jesus has for us—experiencing him personally. When boiled down, many modern disciple making approaches today, if scrutinized, might be seen as inadvertently relying upon a person, a format, a curriculum, or a book—any of which can become a groomsman or bridesmaid in the aisle.

But that, my friends, isn't why Jesus died and rose again. Not by a long shot. The proposal of Jesus is for each of us to enjoy and follow him personally.

To accomplish this, I must constrain myself to do as much as I can in a reproducible manner—in a way that someone with different or lesser gifts or experience can also learn to do.

People were made for this! Jesus wants them to join him in disciple making. While you are showing them how, they'll start throwing logs on their own spiritual fire and become less dependent upon you—this is a win-win. What's more, this value of leaving footprints to follow can be applied across every ministry context.

Embracing this truth dramatically influenced both the depth of participation in our D-groups and Lifegroups and our effectiveness at multiplying both. Doing so is essential to creating the disciple making culture we want, and that's why it's our third core value:

We leave footprints for others to follow.

CHAPTER 5

THE ORIGIN OF THE THREE VALUES

1. WE ARE JESUS-CENTERED.
2. WE HAVE A KINGDOM CALLING.
3. WE LEAVE FOOTPRINTS FOR OTHERS TO FOLLOW.

If these disciple making values were only the fruit of personal lessons I've learned, their value would be limited. They might be good for me, but there might be other values more meaningful to you. What makes these three universally valuable in disciple making is that they are root so deeply in Jesus' scriptural strategy.

What makes these values universally valuable to reproducible disciple making is that they are the ones Jesus specifically gives.

At the risk of losing your attention by being the 1,000th guy to use the Great Commandment and the Great Commission, let me use these two passages to illustrate something. Here they are so you don't have to go find your Bible:

"The most important commandment," answered Jesus, "is this: 'Hear, O Israel: The Lord our God, the Lord is one. Love the Lord your God with all your heart and with all your soul and with all your mind and with all your strength." (Mark 12:29-30)

Then Jesus came to them and said, "All authority in heaven and on earth has been given to me. Therefore go and make disciples of all nations, baptizing them in the name of the Father and of the Son and of the Holy Spirit, and teaching them to obey everything I have commanded you. And surely I am with you always, to the very end of the age." (Matthew 28:18-20)

THE GREAT COMMISSION AND THE GREAT COMMANDMENT ARE JESUS-CENTERED

If we look at these with a careful or even a cursory eye, we find they are entirely Jesus-centered. After all...

- Who are we supposed to love with all that we are? *Jesus.*
- To whom has all authority been given? *Jesus.*
- Of whom are we to make disciples of all nations? *Jesus.*
- In whose name are we to baptize? *Father, Son Jesus, and Holy Spirit.*
- Who are we to obey and to teach others to obey? *Jesus.*
- Who is with us always? *Jesus.*

Both the passages we refer to as the Great Commandment and the Great Commission are entirely Jesus-centered. Everything flows out of this priority. There may be a thousand implications and a thousand ways to express the impact of this truth on our lives, but a way to state it in its simplest form is some version of this: We are Jesus-centered.

THE GREAT COMMISSION AND THE GREAT COMMANDMENT EXPRESS OUR KINGDOM CALLING

When we examine the Great Commission, our Kingdom calling nearly hits us square in the face. "Go and make disciples of all nations..." The whole reason behind making disciples of Jesus is to expand his Kingdom.

As I said previously, it's not a "have to," it's a "get to." Our Kingdom calling is what differentiates us from the world. I'm not living to build my kingdom, but Jesus' Kingdom. No longer am I held captive to a life of futility—eat, drink, for tomorrow we die[11]—now my life matters beyond anything I deserve.

The "have to" versus "get to" motivation presents a good opportunity for me to add a word about Jesus' method of expanding his Kingdom. Because Jesus is God, in the strictest sense of the word, he doesn't need anything, including us. But in his sovereign will, he has chosen to work incarnationally, first by becoming man himself and then by indwelling men and women who receive him as Lord and Savior.

He has chosen to work with and through his followers in almost everything he does. Was he obligated to operate this way? No, he's God. Was he too weak to build his Kingdom without us? No, again, he's God. He is not encumbered by obligation or weakness. He chose to include us—to give us this Kingdom calling—for one reason and one reason alone: he *desires* us.

God chose to include us—to give us this Kingdom calling—for one reason and one reason alone: he *desires* us.

The greatest evidence for this is the Great Commandment. God's first priority for us isn't to work harder, be more intense, or more radical. If it were, he would have said so. Instead, the Greatest Commandment is to love him with everything we've got.

It is essential to understand that God doesn't need us but he desires

11 Isaiah 22:13

us. Answering the Kingdom calling under the mistaken notion that God *needs* us always results in collateral damage. I'm not saying that we won't participate in the Kingdom expansion, but generally, it will result in unnecessary cost, hardship, burnout, or hurt. Many people throughout history (including not a small number of lead pastors like myself) have put undue pressure/expectation/condemnation—choose your own word here—on themselves, those they love, and those they lead. Following a person who is driven by an underlying sense that God needs them can be draining/disheartening/devastating or _____ . (Again, I'll let you insert your own word here).

Conversely, when we answer the Kingdom call like the bride who knows that she is deeply desired and wanted, we are far more likely to experience fruit and freedom. By *fruit,* I mean people learning to enjoy and follow Jesus together in a way that we can show others how to enjoy and follow him too. By *freedom,* I mean less hindered by sin, lies, and wounds of the past. This is a great way to live.

When we live out our Kingdom calling in response to the Groom's deep desire to include us, we find that the yoke really is easy and the burden is genuinely light. We don't sacrifice progress in the Kingdom under his yoke; rather, we experience more of the fullness of God's Kingdom because it not only expands through us but also within us.

THE GREAT COMMANDMENT AND THE GREAT COMMISSION LEAVE FOOTPRINTS FOR OTHERS TO FOLLOW

While the Great Commission leaves room for all kinds of creative expression and execution, it also puts an obvious demand upon us. Within the warp and woof (ask your grandmother) of the Great

Commission is the distinct element of reproducibility. We are to teach new disciples to obey everything Jesus has commanded, including the Great Commission itself so that these new disciples might themselves become disciple makers. We must, therefore, do whatever we do in a way that leaves footprints for others to follow.

When we enjoy and follow Jesus, the Kingdom expands, but the yoke is easy and the burden is light.

Again, for those who might initially bristle at the idea of discipling a bit more reproducibly and a bit less intuitively, I promise that your discipline to adopt this third value will be richly rewarded as you see Jesus generously giving you a spiritual family tree beyond anything you'd previously imagined.

Voluntarily constraining yourself to a life-giving, reproducible approach to disciple making makes you an important leg of a relay team in a most important spiritual race.

When I speak of constraint, I'm not referring to following lockstep in some boilerplate template. Again, while that's reproducible, it's not life-giving. I'm talking about embracing the goal of experiencing Jesus personally and some principles that God reveals about how to do so.

THE PRACTICAL VALUE OF THE THREE VALUES

Almost 100% of the time, when a disciple making experience goes bad it's because I violated or neglected one of the Three Values. Look at some of the common mistakes that can contribute to this and see if any apply to you:

- I talked too much (my personal favorite.)
- I didn't manage our time well.

- I didn't rein in an over-talker.
- I didn't have a plan for the D-group.
- I was distracted by my phone. (You can put your phone away while disciple making...Jesus will never text you.)
- I hadn't been enjoying Jesus personally myself. (Yikes!)
- I didn't meet in a quiet place for D-group so focusing on Jesus was hard.
- I never let anyone else lead.
- I focused on information transfer to the neglect of experience.
- I never showed those I was discipling how to hear the Lord for themselves
- There are another hundred I could list.

Do you see how these violate the Three Values? Conversely, can you see how looking through the lens of the Three Disciple Making Values would help you avoid these and other errors?

These Values serve not only to describe the abundant life that Jesus has for you but also as a powerful diagnostic for determining why a disciple making meeting went well or poorly. They are simple, and I use them all the time.

Disciple making is all about enjoying and following Jesus together in a way that allows us to show others how to enjoy and follow him too. Let's jump into what that can look like...

CHAPTER 6

THE CORE EXPERIENCES

"TALKING THEN LISTENING. LISTENING THEN TALKING. THE DANCE STEPS OF RELATIONSHIP."

It was Friday night. I was 16 and just a few hours from taking my now wife, Debbie, on our very first date. We were going to The Loading Zone, a restaurant in Waco, Texas whose menu was based on variations of baked potatoes (unsurprisingly, it went out of business). I was excited about the idea of being with Debbie, but I was also scared to death. I'd known her since I was in the fifth grade and saw her at church all the time, but I was about to be *alone* with her. It was one thing to relate to her in a group of our friends, but to actually be alone with her with no one else to carry the conversation for us was a whole other challenge.

I almost bailed out of nervousness, but my mom talked me down off the ledge. (I owe you one, Mom!) She reminded me that conversation is just like tennis, where you hit the ball back and forth to one another. "One of you will talk," Mom said, "while the other listens. And then you hit the ball over the net and the other person will talk while the other listens." I know this seems utterly basic, but remember, I was just 16 and Debbie's blue eyes were and still are *really* distracting. Mom's advice helped and as a bonus, she shared with me some simple questions I could use to get the conversational tennis game going.

During our teenage years and early 20s, Debbie and I realized that we enjoyed communicating with each other more than any other person on the entire planet (I like to be dramatic). Communicating with Debbie was more fun, more free, more engaging, and more of lots of other things—and it still is! And you know what? Even though we're no longer two teenagers navigating the nuance of conversational exchange at The Loading Zone but instead are empty nesters (Debbie prefers the term free birds), can you guess what everyday relationship still relies upon?... wait for it...wait for it...Yes, our decades-old friendship still relies upon communication—talking and listening to one another.

Friendship and communication are a wonderful part of what it means to be made in the image of God and created for relationship with him. So many of the principles of human life and human relationships are pointing to the principles of spiritual life and our spiritual relationship with Jesus.

God repeatedly describes our relationship to him as being that of a bride to her Groom (and as a dearly loved child to the best of Fathers).

If good communication—talking and listening—is critical for a healthy marriage, then you can bet there's a parallel truth that applies to our relationship with God...and sure enough, there is. God repeatedly describes our relationship to him as being that of a bride to her Groom (and as a dearly loved child to the best of Fathers). Talking and listening to one another is at the core of these two most important of human relationships. They are also two of the most important experiences of what you might describe as our Vertical Relationship with Jesus.

But don't forget, God is also building a family as he invites people into his Kingdom. In a family, the children learn from the parents how to communicate and relate to each other. The same is true in God's family. Therefore God wants to help us learn to listen to him for the sake of loving others and he wants to help us learn to talk with others about him. These two experiences form our Horizontal Relationship with God and others.

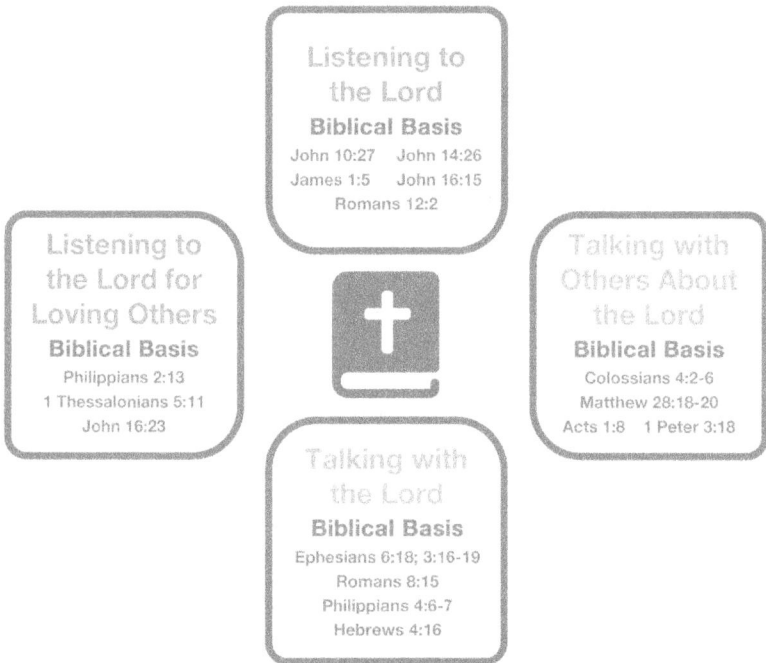

These Core Experiences represent the basics of spiritual communication. While there are no doubt myriad experiences we can and will have with the Lord, the four listed here are the irreducible minimums, the building blocks of a spiritual relationship with Jesus.

The two in the center of the diagram represent the core of our

These Core Experiences equip us to enjoy and follow Jesus for the rest of our lives and into eternity.

fellowship with Jesus—our vertical relationship. The two on the sides represent the horizontal relationship we share with Jesus and others.

Does a Christian need more than these? Absolutely, but you cannot access the "more" if you don't have these basics down. These Core Experiences equip us to enjoy and follow Jesus for the rest of our lives and into eternity. When we neglect these experiences, we inevitably wind up de-personalizing our relationship with Jesus. When that happens, we cease to enjoy him, and if we don't enjoy him, we won't follow him—at least not when the going gets tough.

WE WANT THIS BECAUSE WE WERE MADE FOR THIS

Most followers of Jesus already have a sense that these Core Experiences are an essential part of their spiritual lives. My experience has shown that even if a person I'm discipling doesn't use the precise terms I've used in my chart, they still have a longing for the experiences these terms describe.

They want to feel close to Jesus, to know his will, to recognize his spiritual voice, and to sense his personal presence, comfort, and encouragement.

Similarly, every person I've ever discipled dearly hoped that prayer could be less one-sided and something more enjoyable than simply dropping their list of requests on God's celestial doorstep.

The same is true regarding the two experiences that undergird the horizontal relationship we share with Jesus and others.

Jesus designed us with a desire for Kingdom significance. We *want* to bless others and *want* Jesus to include us in loving others.

And even though we often mistake sharing the good news of Jesus with someone as a "have to" instead of a "get to," that's not how we want it to be. In fact, we want-to-want-to.

It's true that our sinful nature and our spiritual enemy often get in our way, but my point is that when the Holy Spirit takes up residence in a person, we are instantly able to experience Jesus in these ways. His Spirit within us stirs up a holy sense of desire and anticipation for more because Jesus is infinitely captivating—meaning he will captivate our attention forever. And just like in every other relationship, the more we enjoy Jesus through these experiences, the deeper and richer our relationship will be. In fact, it will never stop growing deeper. We're going to get to enjoy Jesus forever as we listen and talk with him and with others who love him too.

So let's talk about how we show someone how to enjoy Jesus in these core ways—and let's remember our two-fold goal:

1. We want to learn to enjoy and follow Jesus together, while at the same time...
2. We want to do it in a way that shows others how to enjoy and follow him too.

CHAPTER 7

EXPERIENCE 1: LISTENING TO THE LORD

"LIKE EVERY GOOD FATHER, JESUS LOVES TO ENCOURAGE AND STRENGTHEN HIS CHILDREN PERSONALLY."

An acquaintance of mine once said to me, "Kirk, you always talk about listening to the Lord. If I want to know what God's saying, I can just go to the Bible."

I understand this sentiment. I believe in the sufficiency of Scripture. The Bible is God's unchanging Truth for all people for all time and sufficient for salvation and a life that glorifies God. That's why in disciple making, we *always* start with Scripture. When we do, we discover that through Scripture, God tells us *explicitly* to expect him to speak to us. God's Word *commands* us to go to God's Spirit directly.

Here are just five of the many—and I do mean many—Scriptural examples of this:

> Listening to the Lord
> **Biblical Basis**
> John 10:27   John 14:26
> James 1:5   John 16:15
> Romans 12:2

[Jesus said,] My sheep listen to my voice; I know them, and they follow me. (John 10:27)

If any of you lacks wisdom, you should ask God, who gives generously to all without finding fault, and it will be given to you. (James 1:5)

All that belongs to the Father is mine. That is why I said the Spirit will receive from me what he will make known to you. (John 16:15)

Do not conform to the pattern of this world, but be transformed by the renewing of your mind. Then you will be able to test and approve what God's will is—his good, pleasing and perfect will. (Romans 12:2)

When the Father sends the Advocate as my representative—that is, the Holy Spirit—he will teach you everything and will remind you of everything I have told you. (John 14:26 NLT)

Could God be any more specific or clear? He's inviting us into a *personal* relationship with him. Let's take him up on his generous offer! That's the whole point of the incarnation.

How disappointing it would be to think that Jesus came to earth in the likeness of man to reveal God to us by walking, talking, teaching, laughing, eating, and celebrating with people, only to then retreat inaccessibly to Heaven. We're now his tabernacle, his meeting place. He wants to relate to us now! He wants us to know, sense, perceive, and understand his spiritual voice now—and we can!

BUT IS IT SAFE?

Most of the time when I show people how to Listen to the Lord, they are deeply moved by how accessible Jesus is and how readily he affirms his love to them. I've also had people come to me and say, "This feels really safe when I'm with you, but if we teach people that any Christian can "hear" God, then don't we risk opening up a Pandora's Box of heresy?"

We *always* start with Scripture.

This is a really good question and would be a valid concern except for the fact that God has given us a way to test and approve what we believe to be from him.[12] I can illustrate this by introducing you to Big Daddy.

Big Daddy was the name we called my maternal grandfather, and Big Daddy raised sheep. Actually, he was a business entrepreneur, who started a grocery distribution company in the 1930s, driving trucks from the big city of Beaumont to small town communities nearby, but he later owned some ranches in the Texas hill country where he raised sheep.

The summers of my childhood (think *That 70s Show)* included weeks at my grandparents' ranch with Big Daddy and his wife, whom I referred to as Big Mama. I usually enjoyed getting to "help" Big Daddy with various ranch jobs. I say "usually" because there was one job that made me want to run and hide: mending fences. Unfortunately, this was also one of the most common jobs that needed doing.

The help I rendered generally consisted of my standing in the heat of the Texas summer, handing Big Daddy u-shaped fencing staples that he used to secure barbed wire to the fence posts. My role was the epitome of what we call unskilled labor. It was the most boring part of one of

---

12 Romans 12:2 reveals the promise that God has made a way for us to reliably discern his will, if what we're hearing is actually his spiritual voice.

Sheep need a pasture and fences are what make a pasture. the most tedious ranch jobs as we side-stepped down, stopping every eight feet to tap in the staple over the barbed wire onto the post along a fence line that seemed to stretch all the way to Mexico.

I remember complaining and asking Big Daddy why we had to check every single fence post. His reply: "Sheep need a pasture and fences are what make a pasture. Without it, sheep'll get into all kinds of trouble."

When it comes to knowing God's will and discerning his spiritual voice, God provides the followers of Jesus a pasture. It's a three-sided pasture with three corner posts:

1. The Word of God.
2. The Spirit of God.
3. The People of God.

Drawn simply, the pasture might look like this:

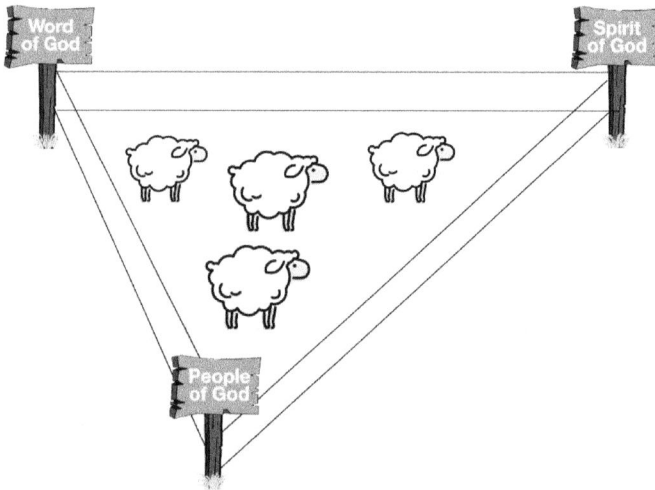

All three of the posts are required to form the pasture. Without any one of the three posts, the pasture disappears.

The Word of God, the Bible, is God's infallible, beautiful, and perfect expression of his will and ways. It is true, being universal in its application and eternal in its scope. To give credit to the acquaintance I referenced as I opened this chapter, if we want to know God's will, we can and should look to the Bible—it's one of the critical fenceposts forming our pasture. When we look to the Word of God, we will find that God encourages us to rely upon the Spirit of God. This makes sense—after all, the reward of the resurrection is an actual personal relationship with the living God forever. We can begin enjoying this forever relationship now.

When the Spirit of Jesus (aka Spirit of God, Holy Spirit, Holy Ghost) speaks, we can confirm that we're discerning his spiritual voice correctly because:

1. **He always speaks consistently with the Word of God.** Jesus will never contradict what he's already told us in his Word, the Bible. He will always be perfectly consistent. Isn't it good to know he's safe like that?

2. **He always speaks with the tone and character of a good Father.** Good fathers are strong, gentle, wise, encouraging, and exhorting. They don't threaten or frighten their children.

3. **He always speaks in a positive, not condemning tone** (even though his words may be convicting).[13] Jesus died specifically to take away condemnation. Even when the Holy Spirit is convicting me of sin, his tone isn't condemning, it's often strong, urgent, and persistent, but not condemning. Thank you, Jesus!

---

13 I first heard points 2 and 3 articulated by my friend Rick Bewsher and when I did, I felt chains of condemnation fall off me that have never burdened me since.

4. **He always speaks in a way our Christian community can affirm or correct.** To have confidence in what we're sensing from the Lord, we need to be walking in ongoing community. (More on this in a moment.)

The Holy Spirit loves to wield his sword (the Word of God) in our lives. Because he cares for us and actually enjoys relating to us, the Spirit of God takes the unchanging Word of God and speaks it to us personally, applying it to our situation, making it real and timely. Bible study is, of course, wonderful and essential (do me a favor and read that again), however, we cannot understand the Word nor can we apply it correctly, if we rely upon our intellect alone. And besides, who would want to settle for the conclusions of their own finite mind anyway? Jesus wants to share

When we find agreement within the Word of God, the Spirit of God, and the People of God, we can know we are hearing the Lord accurately.

his thoughts with us. God even promises that we have the mind of Christ.[14] Eternal life starts the moment we trust in Christ. And what is eternal life? Knowing the Father and Jesus Christ whom he has sent. How do we know him? Through the Holy Spirit.

Knowing him will be so much more natural and fun in heaven and on the new earth, but we can know him right now too. This is what Jesus was both preaching and modeling for us when he retreated to lonely places.

The wonderful reality we have available to us right now is that we can know Jesus' love in a way that surpasses mere knowledge. We can

---

14 1 Corinthians 2:16

know it experientially to a degree that can only be described as being filled to the full measure of God.[15] But he has even more for us...

Because God is creating a family, he loves to include his children in blessing his children, which brings us to the third fence post of the spiritual pasture.

TWO POSTS DON'T MAKE A PASTURE

The final fencepost that secures our pasture is the people of God.

Sometimes the instability of our souls makes it hard for us to trust that we're hearing the Lord accurately and may shake our interpretation of his Word. Fortunately, God is our Father and he's brought us into a family filled with his other children, our spiritual brothers and sisters. Despite the tendency of American culture to value independence over many other things, life in a family is characterized by mutual dependence. So it is in God's family—and always has been. Just think about to whom the New Testament epistles were written. Paul reminds his reader, "Not many of you were wise by human standards, or influential, or of noble birth."[16] There wasn't a surplus of seminary graduates in the first century who were standing over the normal folk telling them how to determine God's will. In fact, when "Christian" religious education became institutionalized, it took 1,200 years and the Reformation to overcome it. My point isn't to bash seminary grads (I am one), but rather to remind us all that God's plan has always been for us to test and approve his will through the Word of God, the Spirit of God, and the People of God. It's his way.

When we find agreement with these three, we can humbly but confidently know that we're discerning the spiritual voice of Jesus accurately. No good father withholds good things from his child. Rather,

---

15 Ephesians 3:18-19

16 1 Corinthians 1:26-29

he gives them what he knows they need. A good father's heart desires to provide, care, encourage, and comfort—and we have the best of Fathers.

THE STARTING POINTS FOR LEARNING TO LISTEN TO THE LORD

It might be helpful at this point to re-read the story I shared about Leo. In it, I describe three Starting Points—three simple, reproducible activities to help a person begin to listen to the Lord.

Starting Points are simply that: places to start. Just like a map is really helpful the first time a person travels a route, the more familiar the route becomes, the less the map is needed. Don't make the Starting Points a set of rules. They are simply reproducible ways to show a person how to begin to enjoy and follow Jesus.

Graphically the Starting Point for Listening to the Lord looks like this:

After Leo and I had shared a Discovery Bible Study (DBS), we used "I want you to know" as a Starting Point for listening to the Lord.

> **Listening to the Lord**
> **Starting Point**
> Discovery Bible Study
> "I want you to know..."
> "I will..." statement

If you re-read the story you'll remember that Leo heard or sensed the Lord impressing these encouraging words upon him: *Leo, I want you to know that I'm really glad that you want to know more about me. I've been wanting this for a long time. If you'll keep reading the Bible you'll get to know me more.*

Leo and I had no trouble testing and approving what he'd heard by looking at Scripture and the character of God. It's not surprising that God expressed delight and eagerness at Leo's desire to know him more—all good daddies feel this way toward their children.

Now, is it possible that Leo might have heard something that actually *wasn't* from the Lord? Could Leo have written something that might

have actually been heresy? Of course. But remember that if heresy was already in Leo's heart or mind, this Starting Point brings heresy or misunderstanding of God's will into the light where we could actually deal with it, testing it against and correcting it with the good news of God's Truth.

This Starting Point brings heresy or misunderstanding of God's will into the light where we could actually deal with it.

When a person learns to Listen to the Lord, they'll discover how gentle and reassuring Jesus is. He always says things that penetrate far deeper than what a groomsman or bridesmaid might say. This isn't to say that Jesus doesn't speak through people, it's just that he seems to enjoy saving the extra special things to say for himself. He loves the time when it's just you and him.

The lack of understanding of how to hear the Lord personally could be one of the reasons two-thirds of kids who grow up in Christian homes and in the church wind up leaving their faith for at least a year after high school.[17] Could it be that these kids have had plenty of "church" and plenty of coaching in what they were supposed to do and not do, but they never actually experienced Jesus personally? When a person discerns the spiritual voice of the Lord, everything changes. When people recognize Jesus as real and attentive and encouraging, why would they ever leave him?

That's why Listening to the Lord is one of the most important Core Experiences in disciple making.

---

17 Lifeway Research. "Reasons 18- to 22-Year-Olds Drop Out of Church." Accessed September 4, 2024. https://research.lifeway.com/2007/08/07/reasons-18-to-22-year-olds-drop-out-of-church.

THE JOY OF THE DISCIPLE MAKER

Before we move on to the second of our Core Experiences, let me reiterate something I mentioned in my story with Leo: That day was the best day of my week! Can you imagine how fantastically generous of Jesus it was to include me in helping Leo experience him for the first time?! (Not to mention teaching him how to say Zak-ē-us.)

Perhaps most amazing of all was that it was easy! As a groomsman, I stayed next to Jesus and out of the aisle, and guess what?… Jesus drew Leo to him. It was amazing! I couldn't wait to share it with my wife…and my kids…and our staff team…and anyone else who would listen. That night I went to bed high-fiving Jesus!

This is just one example of the kind of rich moments included in a life of disciple making. I've got so many more—and you will too when you say "Yes!" to Jesus' Kingdom calling for your life and learn to disciple your kids and others all while leaving footprints behind for them to follow. In fact, I can't resist. Here's one more quick story…

When one of our daughters, was in 4th grade she came home from school distraught. A classmate of hers had made fun of her glasses and the tendency of one of her eyes to bend inward. I was learning about this when I was sitting on her bed saying goodnight. Part of our bedtime routine (thanks to Brian Hannas) was to ask our girls at bedtime a simple but important question: Did anyone hurt your heart today? (Many of the lies we tell ourselves as adults began in our childhood. Well-timed questions like this one can help parents extract the arrows that get stuck in our kids' hearts before they infect their identity. More on this later.)

I have to admit that when my daughter shared this wound she'd been dealt by a boy in her class, my knee-jerk response wasn't very holy. I wanted to say something like, "Sweetheart, that boy is an idiot, just like his dad!" (I resisted.) Another possible response that came to mind,

Why don't we ask Jesus what's true?

and one a bit more holy than the first, was for me to tell her something encouraging, "Don't listen to that boy, your eyes are beautiful." While there would have been nothing wrong with my saying that—and girls dearly need their dads to encourage them—there was an even better option. That's the one I chose. "Sweetheart, I know that boy made fun of you, but why don't we ask Jesus what's true?"

This wasn't new for us so we closed our eyes and I said, "Jesus, my girl's heart is hurting, do you have anything you want to say to her?"

We waited in silence for a few moments and then I opened my eyes and asked her, "What did Jesus say to you?"

She looked at me and smiled, "Jesus said he likes my eyes."

She had heard Jesus, and if you'd seen my daughter's face you'd have known that she believed what Jesus had just said. How sweet and kind Jesus is!

This moment with my daughter illustrates why learning to listen to the Lord is so important. What my 10-year-old heard from Jesus was simple—in fact, it sounded quite similar to what had come to my mind to say to her. But remember, even though I'm her dad, in another sense I'm also a groomsman. My role is to create the context for her to experience Jesus—which I did by suggesting we ask Jesus what's true. When Jesus said those simple words, "I like your eyes," they went to a deeper place in her heart than my words could ever have gone. (Of course, I got to agree with Jesus and told her I like her eyes too.)

When people experience Jesus encouraging them, guiding them, or reminding them of what's true, it's a game changer. They transcend mere religious discipline and begin to move into a new place of enjoying him personally. That's why Listening to the Lord is the first of our Core Experiences.

CHAPTER 8

EXPERIENCE 2:
TALKING WITH THE LORD

"WHEN PEOPLE EXPERIENCE JESUS, EVERYTHING CHANGES."

For most all my life, I knew that prayer was vitally important to the Christian life. I also knew that I was supposed to pray. But I had two problems: Prayer seemed boring and so I didn't want to pray. It's really hard to do something consistently if you don't enjoy it and you don't see the purpose in it—such was my experience with prayer. This isn't to say that I never prayed...I just never prayed very much.

Honestly, I found prayer logically confusing. If God knew everything already, and if God was going to do whatever he wanted to do, why did I need to invest time praying when there were a million other things I could be doing?

What made prayer even more puzzling for me were some of the strange, seemingly unobtainable promises Jesus

> Talking with
> the Lord
> **Biblical Basis**
> Ephesians 6:18; 3:16-19
> Romans 8:15
> Philippians 4:6-7
> Hebrews 4:16

and others made in the Bible. See if you can relate to my struggle as you read these verses:

> I will do whatever you ask in my name, so that the Father may be glorified in the Son. You may ask me for anything in my name, and I will do it. (John 14:13-14)

> Whatever you ask in my name the Father will give you. (John 15:16b)

> Very truly I tell you, my Father will give you whatever you ask in my name…Until now you have not asked for anything in my name. Ask and you will receive, and your joy will be complete. (John 16:23b-24)

> This is the confidence we have in approaching God: that if we ask anything according to his will, he hears us. And if we know that he hears us—whatever we ask—we know that we have what we asked of him. (1 John 5:14-15)

These Scriptures offer fantastic promises…if you can figure out what it means to pray in his name or according to his will. If not, well, you're out of luck, thanks for playing. At least that's what I thought growing up. And because this is what I thought, I figuratively put prayer on the shelf. I didn't throw it away, but I placed it on the spiritual shelf of my soul and seldom took it down to use it.

That was until one day as I was reading the Bible, the Holy Spirit connected some previously unconnected dots in my belief system. I believe wholeheartedly that the Word of God is true and right…I believe that it is the authoritative expression of his name—God's will and ways.

What I had missed completely is that when you add those together the Bible is revealed to us as a prayer guide. The whole of Scripture—in one way or another—tells what and how to pray. Discovering Scripture as fuel for prayer was the secret unlocking what seemed to me to be the mystery of prayer!

The Bible is in fact filled with examples of people's prayers. God included them so that Jesus' followers in ages to come might know how to pray and when to pray and why. We simply pray Scripture. I don't mean we recite it—though memorization is powerful—I mean we use it as a launching pad that propels us into a living conversation with Jesus as we learn to talk *with* him.

> We simply pray Scripture...we use it as a launching pad that propels us into a living conversation with Jesus.

Here is a life-giving, reproducible way to do this…I call it Discovery Prayer and it's a simple Starting Point for showing someone how to Talk with the Lord.

Do you remember how in a Discovery Bible Study we read Scripture and then discussed what it revealed about God and what it revealed about people? Discovery Prayer is similar to this. You pick a passage of Scripture and read it slowly a couple of times. Then you ask the Holy Spirit to reveal:

1. What does this passage reveal about God that you can **thank** him for or **declare** about him?
2. What does this passage reveal about Jesus' followers that you can **declare** or **ask** for more of?

Then together you pray using the pattern of Thank-Declare-Ask. It's simple but powerful.

Could a person look at Scripture and make a list of items for which they might Thank-Declare-Ask *without* actually praying? Of course. Sometimes that's a good starting point too. But when people pray together, Jesus meets them. He's with them. He's the one who makes the experience meaningful. The special role of the disciple maker is to help the disciple get started and to show them the way.

Have you noticed that in a wedding the bridal party enters *before* the bride? Typically the groom is first…then the groomsmen and the bridesmaids…and *then* the bride comes. In a ceremonial sense, the groomsmen and bridesmaids create and guard the aisle. They create the context in which the bride will experience the groom.

When people pray together, Jesus meets them.

So it is in reproducible disciple making. The disciple maker creates the context, walking the aisle first and showing the disciple the way to Jesus.

Here's a way to lead someone into the experience of Talking with the Lord. I might pick a passage like Colossians 1:9-10 where Paul prays:

> Since the day we heard about you, we have not stopped praying for you. We continually ask God to fill you with the knowledge of his will through all the wisdom and understanding that the Spirit gives, so that you may live a life worthy of the Lord and please him in every way: bearing fruit in every good work, growing in the knowledge of God.

In Discovery Prayer, as we Thank-Declare-Ask, we follow this simple order:

- We pray.
- We pause.
- We listen.
- (Repeat)[18]

While it's a little challenging to describe this in writing, I or someone with me might pray something like...

Lord God, thank you that you are the God of all knowledge. *(Thank)* You alone possess the knowledge we need. *(Declare)* Your will is the best, Jesus! *(Declare again)* We want it! All that you have for us, we want. Come fill us with the knowledge of your will. *(Ask.)*

Pause and listen: Whether I'm alone talking with the Lord or with my child or in a disciple making group, I don't generally pray long prayers. I pause and listen, giving the Holy Spirit room to direct my thoughts. Oftentimes, he brings other things to mind that lead me to *thank, declare,* or *ask.* I did just that as I was writing this portion and this is what the Holy Spirit stirred up in my mind to pray....

Father, your will is always for the highest good! *(Declare)* I humble myself before your will, relinquishing mine to give way for yours. *(Declare)* I give you my entire life as your workspace, let your Kingdom come first in me and through me, Papa. *(Ask.)*

Perhaps the most important part of this is when I Pause and Listen.

---

18 This pattern is simple, but Pastor Brian Hannas helped me see how important it is to experiencing the Holy Spirit when we pray.

As I do, I'm being sensitive to the whispers of the Holy Spirit just as I was teaching Leo to do when we did that first DBS. It's not magic and it's not self-talk—it's way better than either—it's actually experiencing Jesus just as the Bible promises we can.

To help our church begin to experiment with this, one Sunday I asked them to raise their hand and shout out loud whatever came to mind in response to the phrase "God's will" in Colossians 1:9.

Before we did it, I prayed out loud, "Father God, would you bring to our mind words and thoughts related to your will? Then, we went for it. Yes, it felt a little like a TV game show as hands went up all over and people began to shout out responses like...Good...Big...Eternal... Unstoppable...For our best...Magnificent...Beautiful...Forever (uh, isn't that like eternal?)...Trustworthy...and lots of others.

Then we took literally one minute to say those things directly to God in prayer. Simple, right? Yet we had people tell us it changed the way they looked at prayer and at Scripture.

Since learning Discovery Prayer, talking with the Lord has become one of my favorite things to do. I love to wake up early, while it's still dark, and go walking in my neighborhood. I usually pick a Scripture and begin talking with the Lord. The more I have done this the richer my talking with him has become. Now when I pause and listen, he generally brings to mind something additional but related to what I just prayed. I might respond as in a conversation with another person and say,

"Oh, I hadn't thought of that!" (Whatever it was.)
"Yes, Lord, thank you for that. Please give me more of that too,"
(or give so-and-so more of that).

As with every relationship we have, more time together results in a

The more I enjoy and follow Jesus, the more life-giving my relationship with him becomes.

deeper friendship. The more I enjoy and follow Jesus, the deeper and more life-giving my relationship with him becomes.

Prayer is no longer on the shelf for me. Instead, prayer doesn't consist merely of my dropping my requests on his heavenly doorstep and sort of awkwardly backing away, it's become a living conversation. I pray for different things…I hope for different things. It's still not without its mysteries, of course. After all, we are *talking* to the God of the Universe—but we are talking *with* the God of the Universe. He's with us! He's enjoying us, too! No longer do my prayers feel weak. Now I feel the inner "Amen!" of Jesus cheering me on,

> *Yes, Kirk! You're going the right way. You and I are on the same page! I am working. I am moving. Keep trusting me, you won't be disappointed!*

Remember, Discovery Prayer is just a Starting Point. If you're a bit more of an engineer-type person, you might be tempted to make this "the" way to show someone how to pray. Resist this. The is simply to open a door through which the other person may enter a world of wonderfully, personal ways of interacting with Jesus.

If you lean toward the artistic/intuitive side of things, you could be tempted to dismiss any kind of structure related to interacting with Jesus. But remember, intuition isn't reproducible. You need some way of helping the person you're discipling to begin talking with the Lord. This

Starting Point, and the others, are an attempt to employ the least amount of structure needed in order to be reproducible but without draining the life out of the experience.[19]

So, here's our graphic showing the second of the Core Experiences and the Starting Point we use to show people how to experience Jesus in this way:

Talking with
the Lord
Starting Point
Discovery Prayer
Thank
Declare
Ask

---

19 If you find a better Starting Point to show people how to begin interacting with Jesus through prayer, then go for it. Just make sure it's Jesus-centered, connects your disciple in some way to their Kingdom calling, and leaves footprints to follow. This way your disciple will be able to share it with those they disciple too.

CHAPTER 9

EXPERIENCE 3: LISTENING TO THE LORD FOR LOVING OTHERS

"JESUS LOVES TO INCLUDE US IN ALMOST EVERYTHING HE DOES."

Have you ever had a friend call just to unload something heavy? Maybe you've been in a Lifegroup or small group when someone shared a burden so overwhelming it seemed to be taking over their thoughts and time.

For much of my life, I usually responded to situations like that in one of two ways:

- I'd express empathy (which is good), then quickly jump into giving advice or solutions (not always so good).
- Or I'd respond with something like, "I'll be praying for you," which often really meant, "I'm not sure what to say right now, and I hope things improve before we talk again."

> **Listening to the Lord for Loving Others**
> **Biblical Basis**
> Philippians 2:13
> 1 Thessalonians 5:11
> John 16:23

But there's actually a better way—a way that's more life-giving, more effective, and more glorifying to Jesus.

WITH HIM. BY HIM.

For years, I started each day feeling pressure to do things for God. But as my relationship with Jesus deepened, I realized something important: God isn't primarily interested in what I can do for him—he wants me to do everything with him.

That's not just a nicer way of thinking—it's a whole new way of living.

Philippians 2:13 makes a remarkable promise: "It is God who works in you both to will and to act according to his good purpose." (Here's my paraphrase: The Spirit of God is the one who gives you the desire to do God's will and the power to carry it out.) He shapes our desires to align with his. And then he equips us to actually do it. With him. By him. Not just for him.

With him. By him. Not just for him.

When we embrace that promise, it changes everything.

For instance, Scripture repeatedly exhorts us to encourage one another and build each other up (see 1 Thessalonians 5:11, Hebrews 10:24). Based on Philippians 2:13, we can confidently expect the Holy Spirit to stir our hearts with the desire to encourage, and then to give us the insight to do it well.

So when a friend comes to me with a burden, I don't need to scramble for advice or offer hollow phrases. I can ask Jesus how to encourage them. I can listen for his thoughts.[20] And because I know Jesus's desire is to strengthen, comfort, and encourage, I can test and

---

20 We have the mind of Christ (1 Corinthians 2:16).

Because I know his desire is to strengthen, comfort, and encourage, I can test and approve what I sense from the Lord to be sure it aligns with Scripture.

approve what I sense from the Lord to be sure it aligns with Scripture and will actually build my friend up.[21]

We looked in Chapter 7 at how we can listen to the Lord—how, when we give him room, we can sense him impressing his thoughts on our minds, filled with love and truth. When that happens, it makes sense that some of what he speaks might be meant for others, too.

Think about it: haven't you been the one carrying a burden, and someone contacted you out of the blue and said, "God put you on my heart today"? That's not random—it's Jesus speaking to them, for you.

A SIMPLE STARTING POINT

This isn't complicated. If Jesus speaks—and we can listen—then he may very well speak something that's meant to encourage someone else. We don't need to be clever or impressive. We just need to give God room.

The Starting Point we use for Listening to the Lord for Loving others is called See-Feel-Respond.

SEE

When someone shares a need or struggle, quietly ask, *Lord, would you help me see what You see?* This simple prayer acknowledges His presence and invites His perspective into the moment.

---

21 2 Timothy 3:16; 1 Corinthians 14:3; Romans 12:2

FEEL

Next, ask Jesus to help your heart align with His: *Help me feel what You feel for this person.* This opens us to his compassion—a love deeper than our own—so we respond not out of pity or pressure, but from Christ-like care.

RESPOND

Then ask, *Jesus, how should I respond?* Maybe it's prayer. Maybe it's a word of Spirit-led encouragement, a quiet act of service, or simply being present. Sometimes what you sense may differ from your natural instincts—and that's okay. If your response is grounded in humility and genuine love, it will bear fruit.

Don't be fooled by the simplicity of this Starting Point. Like the powerful prompt: "I want you to know…," simple doesn't mean shallow. When we slow down and make room for God, He is eager to fill that space. As you grow in this practice, you'll find yourself more confident in the Lord's provision. You'll increasingly sense

> Listening to
> the Lord for
> Loving Others
> **Starting Point**
> See
> Feel
> Respond

his presence and his spiritual voice. This is what he wants. He delights in including us in His work—not because He needs us, but because He wants to be with us.

That's the heart of it: God loves doing things with us, including loving others.

CHAPTER 10

EXPERIENCE 4: TALKING WITH OTHERS ABOUT THE LORD

"WHEN PEOPLE EXPERIENCE JESUS, EVERYTHING CHANGES."

Let me bring Leo back into the picture. That day I showed Leo how to listen to the Lord, and I got to share something else with him that rocked his world. I told him that I'd known that I was going to meet him that day in the park. I didn't know I would specifically meet a guy named Leo, but I had a sense that I was going to cross paths with someone who would benefit from hearing that Jesus hasn't forgotten them and that he loves them.

I went on to tell Leo that while I was driving to the park, I'd prayed a simple prayer that I pray every single day, "Jesus, would you include me in what you're doing today?" I call this the Include Me prayer and it's a Starting Point for showing someone how to Talk with Others about the Lord.

> Talking with Others About the Lord
>
> **Biblical Basis**
> Colossians 4:2-6
> Matthew 28:18-20
> Acts 1:8   1 Peter 3:18

Jesus loves to answer the Include Me prayer, because he's made an irrevocable decision to do almost everything he does in the world incarnationally, through us. When I pray the Include Me prayer, I'm saying, "Jesus, I know you are drawing people to yourself. I know you want them to know how loved they are by you. I'd really like to be part of it."

Universally, good dads love to include their kids in what they're doing. When my girls were little, I resolved to never go anywhere alone on the weekends. (I learned this from my dad.) During the week, my schedule was busy, but on Saturday, I had more flexibility. It was the perfect time to show my girls how important they were to me, so I dropped hunting and playing golf for several years and decided to include them in whatever I was doing. To that end, on a Saturday morning when I needed to go to the hardware store, I would call upstairs to the girls, "Who wants to go with daddy to Home Depot?" I admit that I generally sweetened the offer by stopping on the way to get a donut or a special drink at a coffee shop. The girls knew this and so most of the time, my call to them was met with a chorus of "I do! I do!" I L-O-V-E-D that...and so did they. Why did I enjoy time with my girls like that? Was it because I'm just the perfect Hallmark dad? Not by a long shot. I took delight in including my girls in what I enjoyed doing because that's what good daddies do. Father God is the same way—only better. He loves to be with his kids and he loves to include them in significant things.

God loves to be with his kids and he loves to include them in significant things.

The day I met Leo, I'd asked God to include me. As I continued to drive to the park, I listened and sensed Jesus respond, "Okay, Kirk, I will."

God tells us through Paul in 2 Corinthians 5:18 that one of his top priorities is reconciling the world to himself through Jesus. To be reconciled with the God Who Is Love is to come back into a loving relationship with him. In the same breath that Paul is expressing this priority of God, he also tells us that God wants to include us in that adventure. When we learn to ask Jesus to include us in what he's doing, we can expect him to answer that prayer.

When I shared this with Leo, he was blown away. He was even more shocked when I asked him if he wanted to try praying the Include Me prayer during the next week. He had been amazed that God had already been thinking about him before I met him, but even as I shared the backstory with him, it hadn't occurred to him that Jesus might include him in some way.

Leo immediately tried to complicate the opportunity. "I don't really know what to do…or what to say…or how to do it." I explained that none of that was important. The Include Me prayer is completely dependent upon Jesus—the Groom—choosing to include you by presenting an unmistakable opportunity to care for someone else. If Jesus includes us, well, then he does. If he doesn't present the opportunity, then he doesn't. Our role is simply to ask and to be ready to respond.

Our role is simply to ask and then be ready to respond.

Leo committed to pray the Include Me prayer for the next seven days, and we agreed to touch base after that. It turned out Leo couldn't wait that long. Just three days after we met for the very first time, Leo texted me and asked me to call him as soon as I could. I was immediately concerned, knowing that Leo was working to overcome an addiction and might have relapsed. I couldn't have been more wrong.

When I got Leo on the phone, he was ecstatic. Here's how the conversation went:

"Kirk," he said, "You know how I'm in Narcotics Anonymous?"

"Of course," I said, waiting for the bad news.

"Well, I've been praying the Include Me prayer every day like we said, and today...well, today the leader of our group asked if I would share something for the inspirational moment that starts every meeting! She's never asked me to be the one to share before and as soon as she asked me, I was like, 'Oh s***, that's the Include Me prayer!!'"

Coarse language notwithstanding, Leo and I celebrated how Jesus had answered his prayer!...how Jesus hadn't forgotten him!...how Jesus was willing to include him even though he was still an addict! It was an amazing moment! And Leo was hooked. He was convinced that Jesus was real and alive and that he wanted to know him personally.

As for me, I was the groomsman standing right next to Jesus when he set Leo's heart on fire. There's no other place I'd rather have been.

I was the groomsman standing right next to Jesus when he set Leo's heart on fire.

The Include Me prayer is just a simple Starting Point that puts a person in a position to experience Jesus. There are lots of other ways to do this, so the method isn't all that important.

However, what is vitally important is that the method needs to be Jesus-centered...focused on our Kingdom calling...and, if we want it to reproduce, we have to leave footprints behind, making it easy for others to follow.

LEVELING THE PLAYING FIELD

When I was a child, the pastor of our church periodically had an "evangelism" emphasis season. (Full disclosure, my dad was my pastor.) There was a time we all wore blue buttons stating, "I found it!" The idea was that people would ask us what we'd found and of course, the right answer as it always is in church was: Jesus.

Each time we had a new emphasis my dad or someone else, who had a larger-than-life personality, would share about how to share the gospel with someone.

Now let me be clear, I'm all for sharing the gospel and I don't think there was anything wrong with these methods. What made it hard for me was that the people who taught evangelism or were brought on stage to share their story of sharing the gospel generally seemed to be extroverts—people who could talk to just about anyone...people who never knew a stranger...you know the type. I thank God for those kinds of people—they can reflect the boldness of Jesus—but, if you weren't one of those people (perhaps more introverted), you might have felt inadequate or like a bit of a failure. You might have even decided that evangelism was for "those" kinds of people but not for you.

Surely the joy of seeing someone choose to trust Jesus isn't reserved for the extroverts; what about the other 50% of people? I had this gnawing sense that there had to be a way to level the playing field so everyone could join in. Surely there had to be a way to have spiritual conversations without being weird. I wasn't mistaken.

Somewhere along the way, I ran into a field-leveling principle called Prayer-Care-Share. It's now one of my favorite Starting Points. (I'm sure others have used the words before; they aren't original to me.) Our team has found this opens the door for every follower of Jesus to talk with others about him. Here's a story of how it happened to me in Indonesia....

JOJO AND JESUS

Debbie and I had been visiting a couple of friends in Indonesia one summer. Because Indonesia is comprised of more than 18,000 islands, it's not uncommon to take short flights to and from some of the larger ones. Once on an island, the primary means of getting around is to hire a scooter taxi. Like an Uber, you use an app to hail a scooter driver... who gives you a helmet the rider before you has just worn...you get on and then you hold on for dear life. (I prefer to do this with eyes closed depending upon traffic and how aggressive my driver is.) This, plus the heat, plus keeping a tight schedule to maximize our time in the country lead to fatigue. By the time we were scheduled to depart for the U.S., we were exhausted. I was actually looking forward to the 11-hour flight and getting a chance to rest, be waited on, and try to catch up on some sleep.

Despite running on fumes, I knew I wanted to give Jesus these last 11 hours, so I grabbed Debbie's hand once we took our seats on the plane and quietly prayed, "Lord Jesus, we give you room on this flight to include us in whatever you're doing."

I think Debbie might have added, tongue in cheek, "But Jesus, we'd also like to rest and watch a movie too." (That's my girl!)

I never get used to how much Jesus honors short, seemingly innocuous prayers. It's good to remember that brief, even weak, prayers are prayed to a powerful God. Sure enough, he showed up.

Debbie and I were in the middle section of a five-seat row. Before long, a woman came walking down the aisle, checked her ticket, and then took the seat to my left. Since we were going to sit three inches from one another for 11 straight hours, I was courteous and asked, "How are you doing today?" Sometimes people answer that question with a grunt or the most minimal verbal response they can give, "Fine, thanks." That plus their body language (like if they immediately stick AirPods in their ears) is a pretty obvious sign that they're polite and will be happy to let you out when you need to go to the bathroom, but don't expect to have a conversation with them. (Part of me was really hoping for this.) But that's not what I got.

The woman responded with more than the minimum. "Whew, I barely made it to the airport because my taxi was late. I'm just glad to be on board. I'm JoJo, by the way," as she extended her hand. I reciprocated, "I'm Kirk and this is my wife Debbie." (I'm not trying to throw Debbie under the bus, but…she gave more of the verbal minimum…I'm just sayin'.)

JoJo not only seemed nice, but she was clearly open to talking. Within a few minutes, I'd learned that JoJo was from New York State and had been on a one-week yoga tour on the island of Bali. I replied that that sounded like a miserable vacation. She laughed and began to tell me about her week. She assured me it had been a blast, but that she was leaving to fly back to the States because her grandfather had had a heart attack while she'd been gone. I asked if they were close. The answer was "yes," and JoJo shared some stories of the significance of her grandad in her life.

Though we had just met, the short back-and-forth of our conversation had extended beyond the initial polite exchange of strangers on a plane. She'd shared a concern about something important to her. I'd shown that I genuinely cared by listening intently and actively to her. This context made me feel comfortable and even compelled me to

Would you be okay if I prayed a short prayer for your family right now?

say, "JoJo, I'm sorry to hear about your grandfather's health. I know that's important to you. I believe it's also important to God. Would you be okay if I prayed a short prayer for your family right now?"

This wasn't me being pushy. Nor was it me working to "make something happen." This was me simply staying in step with Jesus as he included me in JoJo's life. JoJo's response was clear evidence of this as her eyes became a bit tearful and she said, "Thank you, Kirk, I would really like that."

And so I prayed. Nothing eloquent or long, just a short, simple prayer to the God of the Universe thanking him for caring for JoJo's family and asking him to remind her that she is precious to him.

After I said, "Amen," I said, "JoJo, there was a time in my life when our oldest daughter was diagnosed with an eye disorder. We didn't know if it was cancer or something else. We had no idea how serious it was. But we read in the Bible where God says that he is a shield around those who trust him.[22] Debbie and I took our concern to Jesus and told him that we were going to trust him with our daughter. She's doing fine now, but even before we knew what the prognosis for her was, we felt a sense of God's peace and presence. Have you ever experienced something like that?" (This is a Starting Point we call the 15-second Testimony.)

JoJo, who'd been listening intently now had a few more tears in her eyes as she replied, "No, but I think it's exactly what I'm looking for."

---

22 Psalm 3

There's more to JoJo's story which I'll share in a moment, but let me pause and zoom out to look at this from a reproducible disciple making perspective. Here's a bullet-point summary of what has transpired up to this point:

- I **prayed** the Include Me prayer giving Jesus room to include Debbie and me in whatever way he chose.
- I **cared** for the stranger next to me, initially by simply asking, "How are you doing?"—a completely appropriate greeting that didn't require gobs of courage. (Good news for introverts, right?)
- JoJo responded in a way that required a simple response from me which led to a conversation that I didn't force or contrive.
- During our conversation, I showed I **cared** by listening and asking follow-up questions. (These are also simply good social skills, by the way.)
- At some point, JoJo **shared** a concern in her life.
- I expressed condolences **(care)** and asked if I could pray for her.
- After I prayed, I **shared** a super short, 15-second Testimony, a story of how Jesus had made a difference in my life when I had a family concern.
- I asked JoJo if she'd ever experienced anything similar in her own life.

It's important to note that I wasn't driving this conversation anywhere, I was just keeping in step with the Holy Spirit. If the conversation hadn't gone beyond my initial greeting, then great—I had greeted her out of obedience to and love of Jesus.

If she'd told me about her grandfather, but politely declined my offer of prayer, no worries. My goal wasn't to get JoJo to some point of decision. My goal was to stay in step with the Holy Spirit. This is always a success for me: Staying in step with the Holy Spirit and only going as far as he leads me. This is the secret to the yoke being easy and the burden being light and it's the secret to enjoying and following Jesus.

But in this case, the Holy Spirit was taking us further. Back to the story...

JOJO AND JESUS PART II

JoJo expressed an interest in knowing more about how to experience God. So I told her,

> Someone shared a picture with me that helped me understand how much God loves me. Could I share it with you?

She was both open and intrigued by this idea and so, on a United Airlines napkin, I drew a picture that expressed our separation from God and how Jesus' death and resurrection create a bridge reconciling us to God.[23]

When the drawing was complete, it showed a person on the left side having been reconciled to God and another person on the right side still separated from God. "Where do you think you are in this picture, JoJo?" I asked. "

"I'm this person," she replied, pointing to the person on the right side. "But I'd like to be here," she said, pointing to the one reconciled to God.

After some more conversation about the drawing, JoJo expressed a desire to follow Jesus and, with a little guidance, she did exactly that. But the thrill didn't end there...

I shared with JoJo that Jesus told a story once that illustrates how he takes care of those who trust and love him and what they can expect from him.

---

23 Though you've likely seen a picture similar to the one to which I'm referring, all of the iterations I've seen are a little different. You can find a video of the Bridge illustration at DiscipleMakingThreads.com.

"Because Jesus was talking with a bunch of rural folks, he likens himself to a shepherd and to those who trust him as sheep," I said.

"And just like sheep recognize the call of their shepherd, Jesus said that his sheep could hear his voice and would follow him."[24]

Then I surprised JoJo a bit by asking her if she would like to listen to see if Jesus had anything to say to her right then. Even though she wasn't expecting this, she was willing to try it. So guess what we did?... Exactly what Leo and I had done...a DBS on Luke 19 about Zacchaeus...and then on the back side of the gospel napkin, I had her write, "JoJo, I want you to know..."

So what did Jesus say to JoJo?

"JoJo, I want you to know that you are way harder on yourself than I am. I love you."

Like Leo, JoJo had heard something that would never have entered her mind previously. But was it really Jesus, she wanted to know?

Rather than reassure her that it was, like a good groomsman, I pointed her back to the interaction between Jesus and Zacchaeus. *"I often condemn myself the way the crowd criticized Jesus for eating with Zatch-us,"* she said, not having mastered the pronunciation quite yet.

I responded enthusiastically, "Yeah! That does fit with what Jesus said to you!" Jesus wasn't criticizing Zacchaeus, and he wasn't criticizing JoJo and he wanted *both* of them to know it.

All of this happened within the first 30 minutes of our 11-hour flight! Jesus is always generous when our heart is calibrated with his passion for disciple making, but sometimes he's *extra* generous.

---

24 John 10:27 is the story Jesus told, but the principle is expressed in lots of others places in the Bible as I've already shown.

THROUGH THE LENS OF PRAYER-CARE-SHARE

If you look at my conversation with JoJo through the lens of Prayer-Care-Share, you'll see a pattern that's easy to reproduce:

Prayer
- Include Me prayer: I prayed this as I got on the airplane.

Care
- Initiate: I greeted JoJo in a normal, non-weird way.
- Listen: I showed I cared by listening about her grandfather.
- With Leo I used The Miracle Question.

Share—Here are some things I shared:
- Prayer—I asked JoJo if I could pray for her situation.
- My story—I shared a 15-second testimony (I followed up by asking JoJo if she'd ever experienced anything like my experience with Jesus.)
- God's story: The Gospel picture on the napkin
- (I ended by asking JoJo which stick person represented where she was in relation to God.)

What's most amazing to me about this Starting Point is how it levels the playing field, allowing Jesus room to give people of different personalities a Kingdom story.

Because it starts with the Include Me prayer, it's completely dependent upon God's actually including us in what he's doing. For years now I've had extroverts *and* introverts come to me excited to share their story of how God included them.

THE OIKOS MAP

Another simple but powerful Starting Point is an Oikos Map. This is a simple, visual way to shine a light on the people within your sphere of influence. These are people with whom you relate in the normal activities of life. Your neighbors, your coworkers, your friends, the barista at your coffee shop, the other regular customers, or the parent you sit next to at your kid's soccer game. All of these are part of your oikos. These are the people in whose lives Jesus is most likely to include you.

The picture below shows an example of an Oikos Map. Once you have created one for yourself, begin a little Prayer-Care-Share to give Jesus room in these relationships. Ask him to include you as he wants. Commit to be willing when the opportunity is presented.

I can all but guarantee that if a person employs this strategy for 30 days, they're going to experience Jesus' including them and, when they do, they'll be hooked.

Remember, disciple making is about learning to enjoy and follow Jesus together in ways we can show others. It's supposed to include fun moments like these.

Here are the Starting Points for Talking with Others about the Lord along with the other Core Experiences:

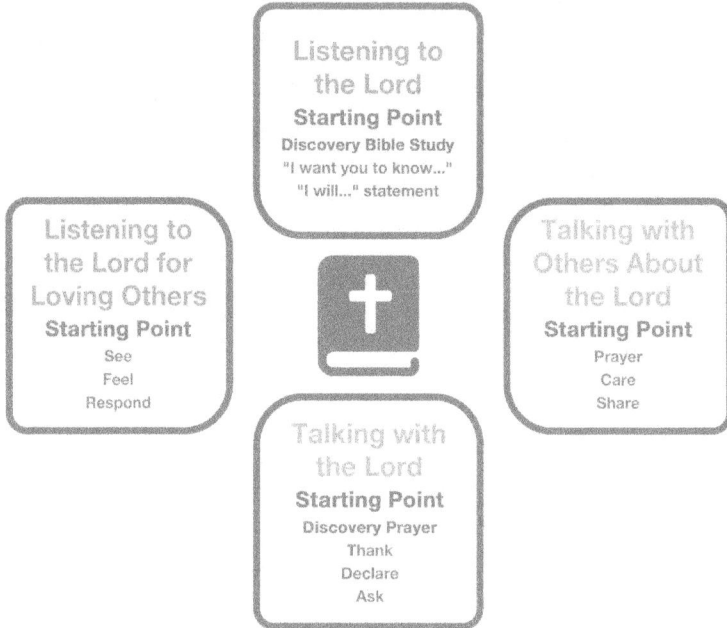

Listening to the Lord

Starting Point

Discovery Bible Study
"I want you to know..."
"I will..." statement

Listening to the Lord for Loving Others

Starting Point

See
Feel
Respond

Talking with Others About the Lord

Starting Point

Prayer
Care
Share

Talking with the Lord

Starting Point

Discovery Prayer
Thank
Declare
Ask

CHAPTER 11

LISTENING TO THE LORD FOR FREEDOM

"METHODS WILL BY NECESSITY CHANGE OVER TIME. VALUES NEVER DO."

If the goal of disciple making includes enjoying and following Jesus, then you can bet that our spiritual enemy is going to come against these in every way he can.

Once, when I was teaching a series over several weeks on the Father Heart of God, I could tell that this truth was really striking a chord with the people in attendance. But at the end of the series, a woman pulled me aside with tears in her eyes. I'm a bit embarrassed to say that I was expecting her to express how grateful she was for this teaching, but instead, she told me how the series had been the hardest for her to sit through in her whole life. Hearing each message was painful, and it had taken everything in her to not leave in the middle of each and just as much strength to come back the next Sunday. This was totally unexpected; I was stunned.

The problem? The memory of the failings and emotional abuse of her earthly father was stirred up every time I characterized God as a father. The wounds of the past were filling her present in a painful way, inhibiting her ability to enjoy God as he has described himself.

She shared further how her earthly dad had demeaned and denigrated her. "You're worthless! No man is ever going to want you!"… and other horrible lies. These harsh, careless comments from her father had festered in her heart since childhood and blossomed into a deadly garden of ungodly beliefs about herself that she was projecting upon Father God. No wonder my series was painful for her! But there was more.

Unsurprisingly, growing up with these wounds and ungodly beliefs had influenced not just what she thought about God and herself, but they had also influenced her personal decisions. Feeling worthless for years, she had engaged in whatever the world promised would give her worth. The result? Shame, guilt, regret, and all the other fruit of sin—all of which were like boulders in her path, keeping her from God.

This one woman's story reflects three of the most universal obstructions to a person's enjoying and following Jesus:

- Wounds
- Ungodly beliefs
- Sin

Our spiritual enemy never stops trying to leverage these three—and others—against us. His goal is to steal our freedom and to do anything he can to make us feel unworthy, guilty, and distanced from God.

We are in a battle with a ruthless enemy.

From the moment we are born to the moment we go to be with Jesus, our enemy presses the attack. We are in a battle with a ruthless enemy, but the Word of God tells us that through the blood of Jesus, we have even more powerful weapons that we can use to overcome the power of the wounds, ungodly beliefs, and sin. These weapons are expressed in words that are familiar to most church-going Christians and yet, I fear this familiarity has led many to overlook them, dismissing the powerful spiritual force for good they each bring to the battle for freedom.

Here they are:[25]

ATTACK	SPIRITUAL WEAPON
Wounds	Forgive and Bless
Ungodly Beliefs	Renounce and Receive
Sin	Confess and Repent

FREEDOM FROM WOUNDS

When we acknowledge our wound instead of hiding it or denying it, we bring it before Jesus like a child runs to their parent when they've gotten hurt. As we listen to Jesus, he gives us his perspective and gently takes the wound from us. Our declaration of forgiveness isn't so much a gift we're giving the person who hurt us, but is in reality a salve the Holy Spirit helps us apply to the wounded place in our own hearts. Forgiveness

Forgiveness is a salve the Holy Spirit applies to our wounded hearts.

in this sense isn't for the other person, it's for us and it's both powerful and effective.

---

25 These are borrowed from FreedomPrayer.org.

FREEDOM FROM UNGODLY BELIEFS

Though the woman, whose story I shared earlier, knew at one level that "God loves me," at a deeper level, she believed something that wasn't true: "I'm not worthy of love." Whatever we believe most deeply is the thing that forms our reality.

Whatever we believe most deeply is the thing that forms our reality.

Often the ungodly belief that's taken root in us, stems from a lie that someone spoke to us, as when the woman's dad told her she was worthless. Other times, we come to believe things that aren't true as the result of disappointment, a broken heart, or even a string of successes. Our enemy will leverage anything he can that is in opposition to what God says is true.

When we identify the lie we're believing, we can confront it with the truth of God. We renounce what isn't true, releasing our grip on it, and we receive what the Holy Spirit says is true and consistent with God's Word.

The only way to destroy a lie is with the truth. When we declare our belief in the truth, we are exercising the spiritual authority we have in Jesus. The process isn't complicated, but don't let the simplicity fool you into missing the powerful reality: God's Truth defeats the enemy's lies.

FREEDOM FROM SIN

Imagine yourself on an overnight hike. You're carrying a backpack and have been careful to load it only with things you need for the hike. As you walk the trail, though, you begin to pick up rocks and put them in your backpack. They aren't useful, they're heavy. They don't enhance your journey, they make it harder. They are just added weight, depleting your energy as you trudge up the mountain. That's sin.

No matter how attractive or appealing something may be to our physical senses or perceived emotional needs, sin loads us down with regret, guilt, and shame, all of which inhibit us from enjoying and following Jesus.

Jesus knows that we battle against sin. For the sake of definition, understand sin as the desire to not trust Jesus and instead to go our own way. His death and resurrection accomplished at least three things regarding sin:

- Jesus breaks the curse of sin, making us acceptable to God.[26]
- Jesus gives us the power to resist sin through the Holy Spirit.[27]
- Jesus gives us a way to re-follow him when we sin.[28]

When a Christ-follower knows to run to Jesus with their sin, to confess it, and then to repent—to align their thinking regarding sin with that of Jesus—freedom is won.

It's true that we often make awful messes regarding our lives. We can tangle our lives layering sin upon sin upon sin. Sometimes the knot of this tangle has so many loops or has pulled so tight over time that the pathway to freedom takes more effort, but ultimately freedom is grounded in Christ's finished work and the foundational principles I've described in this chapter. Because of this, when we teach people how to gain and guard spiritual freedom, we equip them to tackle whatever the enemy throws at them. For a basic, step-by-step guide on how to utilize these weapons of freedom check out the Appendix of this book.

I also highly encourage you to read Jennifer Barnett's book, *First*

---

26 2 Corinthians 5:21
27 1 John 4:4
28 1 John 1:9

Freedoms,[29] which will help you win the battle against the enemy's schemes and heal emotional scars. Another powerful book is *Freedom Tools,* by Andy Reese and Jennifer Barnett. Their book is the most effective guide of which I know for training a ministry team to help others in receiving and guarding freedom. Their website (FreedomPrayer.org) is full of great resources and will connect you to people who love to help pastors and leaders create a culture of spiritual freedom in their church.

---

29 Barnett, Jennifer (2021). *First Freedoms.* Brentwood, TN: Him Publications.

CHAPTER 12

THE POWER OF LEAVING FOOTPRINTS

"IF WE LEARN TO LEAVE FOOTPRINTS FOR OTHERS TO FOLLOW, JESUS WILL GIVE US A SPIRITUAL FAMILY TREE WE'LL CELEBRATE IN HEAVEN FOREVER."

We only had about an hour left of sunlight, but 7:00 p.m. was about the only time we could get a reprieve from the summer heat in Texas. This was when my dad would take me fishing. We'd drive over to a three-acre pond that was just about 10 minutes from our house. Dad would park by one of the better fishing holes and we'd pull out our gear from the back of our wood-paneled station wagon (again, ask your grandmother.) This was where I learned to fish.

This was where my dad taught me how to tie a knot so the lure wouldn't fall off...how to cast (and untangle my line)...how to reel in the lure (with a slight twitch every now and then)...how to jerk the line quick when I felt a fish tug on it...and, of course, how to take the fish off the hook so we could throw it back for catching another day. (Learning a practical skill like that is such a great confidence booster for a young boy or girl.)

There's a lot more to fishing than what I've described, but you know that if you don't have these basics down, you're not fishing. Conversely, once you understand the how and why of these Starting Points, a whole world of fishing awaits you. As long as your equipment is handy, you can enjoy fishing wherever you are.

THE BASICS OF ENJOYING JESUS

Once a person knows how to listen to and talk with Jesus *and* how to listen to him for loving others *and* how to talk with others about him, a whole world of spiritual adventure with Jesus is ahead of them.

Do they need more than just these Core Experiences? Of course they do, but if they don't have these four, then they're far more likely to fall into striving and trying harder, or worse…they become religious.

But *with* these four—and a basic understanding of how to study the Bible—they're unstoppable. Jesus becomes their personal discipler! And as long as they keep following him, they'll get to keep enjoying him…and if they learn how to leave footprints for others to follow, Jesus will give them a spiritual family tree they'll celebrate in heaven forever. All of this begins with experiencing Jesus in the four ways that parallel all human relationships. Disciple making isn't rocket science, it's relationship.

Jesus becomes their personal discipler!

I was at a wedding just a few weeks ago. The venue was a beautiful, white barn placed on a carpet of the greenest grass and surrounded by 50-year-old live oak trees. Best of all…the barn was air-conditioned, which is a necessity for June weddings in Texas. The wedding was full of life and joy and all the honor was directed toward Jesus. It was truly one of the most special weddings I'd ever attended. As soon as the vows had been exchanged and all the special exhortations had been shared, this sweet couple was declared husband and wife to the thunderous applause of all their family and friends. But…the applause wasn't the only thing thundering. No sooner had the couple exited than a storm began dropping buckets of rain accompanied by thunder and a show of lightning that is unique to Central Texas.

This wouldn't have been a problem had the power in the barn not gone out. In an instant, the lights and A/C disappeared. So did the hope of the DJ announcing the wedding party and playing the special song for the first dance. Gone was the fun of lighting up a neon sign that had been created with the names of the bride and groom. You never really understand how much you rely on electricity until it's gone, and now it was definitely gone.

Without a doubt, there was initial disappointment and some tears for the bride and groom, but their disappointment was overshadowed and soon replaced by their bigger reality—we are married! With the help of some candles and guests who were amazingly good sports, the barn was filled with laughter and stories and even some dancing (after someone brought in a small generator).

Yes, months of planning had gone awry, but ultimately it didn't matter. Why? Because at a wedding, the only thing that matters is that the bride gets to be with the groom. So it is in disciple making.

CHAPTER 13

C.A.L.L.
A SIMPLE DISCIPLE
MAKING FORMAT

"OUR GOAL ISN'T TO COVER CONTENT AS MUCH AS IT IS TO EXPERIENCE JESUS."

One of the most common questions I am asked is, "What curriculum do I use for my D-group?" Having read this far, my hope is that you now see how that's not nearly as important a question as you might have once thought.

Because all of Scripture is useful for teaching, correcting, rebuking, and training in righteousness[30] and because the Holy Spirit is the Great Discipler, you really don't need a curriculum. You can rely on the Holy Spirit to wield his Sword.

If you want to walk through the book of John—go for it. If you want to take a topical approach to experience Jesus through the foundations of faith—that's a great choice too. Remember, our goal isn't to cover content as much as it is to experience Jesus, giving him room to encounter us.

---

30 2 Timothy 3:16

That being said, it's important to approach a disciple making meeting with a simple, reproducible process, one that leans on the Three Values.

There are lots of formats for disciple making meetings. Whatever format you use, you can easily weave the Core Experiences into the Bible study part of it. One of the formats I like most was created by my longtime friend, Shawn Sullivan. It looks like this:

- **C**elebration
- **A**ccountability
- **L**earn It
- **L**ive It[31]

The **Celebration** is a time of expressing gratitude. It's how we enter his gates with thanksgiving. What are you thankful for? What is Jesus celebrating in your life? Someone shares an Include Me prayer story or an interaction with someone on their Oikos Map. Maybe God's faithfulness was on display in their kids' lives that week as a prayer was answered and that is celebrated with the D-group. Other times we share what Jesus did in us, through us, or around us.

The **Accountability** portion can be for heart or purity issues or commitments to spiritual disciplines. (This is where freedom issues might come into the light.[32]) This is also the perfect time to share how we obeyed Jesus as we followed through on our "I will" statement or our obedience step. The idea in accountability isn't to catch someone failing, but rather to spur them on and affirm their obedience.

It's actually in the **Learn It** portion that we plan to weave in the

---

31 I'm hoping that Shawn will write a book about this, and I'm encouraging him to do so!
32 Refer back to Chapter 11.

Core Experiences (only one per meeting.) We do a DBS and then encounter Jesus in one of the Experiences. This context provides the most consistent opportunity for showing others how to practice the Core Experiences themselves. Growing in all of them over the course of weeks and months builds confidence that Jesus always shows up and sparks a desire in us to do this disciple making thing with others.

The **Live It** section is when we listen for an "I will…" statement. Regularly hearing the Lord direct our next step of obedience and having someone to celebrate or encourage us onward the following week can be life-changing as anyone who has been in a life-on-life discipleship relationship knows. Hearing the Lord invite us to embrace a truth, to do something specific, or to change a behavior is totally different than coming up with our own objectives or personal applications from a bible study. As we conclude each DBS by asking the Lord for our obedience step, the Holy Spirit becomes our teacher and counselor. (He's a much better discipler than I am!)

If we skip the obedience or action step, we miss out on the transformation that comes from following Jesus.

If we skip the obedience or action step, we miss out on the transformation that comes from following Jesus and the impact of our D-group may not extend beyond a stimulating conversation around the Bible. Try modeling this format consistently in a few meetings, but then, as quickly as possible, ask someone in the group to lead the next week. In this way, disciples become disciple makers all along the way.

WRAPPING UP PART I

Most importantly, to be an effective disciple maker, you must personally be enjoying and following Jesus. It's so hard—perhaps impossible even—to guide someone down a path that you've not traveled yourself.

To be an effective disciple maker, you must personally be enjoying and following Jesus.

In America, we often celebrate the wrong things. We might honor someone who's read through the Bible several times or been exposed to lots of Bible studies or sermons over years of their life or attended all of the latest conferences, but Jesus has so much more for us than just information. Jesus wants *you* to know him better.[33] He wants *you* to live an abundant life rather than just talking about it.[34] Stay grounded in the precious Word of God while at the same time obeying it by pressing in closer to the personal relationship Jesus offers.

I said it previously, but I want you to hear this again: The incarnation wasn't a bait-and-switch operation. Jesus didn't come close to us, making God known to us personally, dying on the cross, and resurrecting from the grave only to then make himself inaccessible to us.

He came to close the gap between us forever. Eternal life has already begun for us who have put their faith in him.[35] Say "Yes!" to him, listening and following, talking and enjoying.

When you do, you'll trust him more. You'll be more bold. You'll talk less and listen more. You'll carry with you the aroma of Jesus because you've been with Jesus.

---

33 Ephesians 1:17
34 John 10:10
35 John 17:3

You will find yourself naturally discipling others, even when you're not trying. Sometimes this will be spontaneous and informal. Conversations with people will take a more spiritual turn, not because you're trying harder, but because Jesus is including you. Because you know you're a groomsman/bridesmaid, you'll find yourself going more directly to Jesus when someone comes to you with a problem or for counsel. The personal intimacy you share with Jesus will overflow into every part of your life.

When you commit to disciple making by intentionally investing in the lives of others, showing them how to weave the Core Experiences into their lives and the lives of others, you'll become a spiritual mother or father with a family tree of disciple makers that impacts generations of people and produces fruit that will last for eternity.

Disciple making is a great way to live life!

PART II

FOR PASTORS AND MINISTRY LEADERS

What would it look like if everyone in your church knew how to enjoy and follow Jesus? How powerful would your church be if everyone were growing in their ability to:

- Listen to the Lord.[36]
- Talk with the Lord.
- Listen to the Lord for loving others.
- Talk with others about the Lord.

Imagine if children were raised by parents who viewed themselves as the chief disciple makers in the lives of their kids. Can you envision the health and impact of a church where these Core Experiences were woven like a common thread through every ministry of your church? What if each ministry was designed to give every person a boost in the same direction—a direction that led the bride to experience the Groom?

As a leader, you dream about this. When you consistently weave

---

36 If the idea of Listening to the Lord feels new or you're feeling uncertain about it, read the section in the Appendix titled: More on Listening to the Lord.

threads of disciple making into the fabric of your church, it becomes the reality. I can tell you from personal experience that it's wonderful to be part of a church moving in that direction filled with people who are more captivated by Jesus than their pastor.

I can also tell you that such a paradigm required a significant heart shift in me and the leaders of our church.

CHAPTER 14

BREAKING MY ADDICTION TO SUNDAY MORNING

Jesus was always using parables and imagery to make his point. He would use the crowd's familiarity with shepherds and sheep or with fishing, leveraging their God-given imagination to paint a picture on the canvas of their minds. I think he still enjoys doing that if we're willing to be still and wait.

One morning, years back, after I'd spent some time in the Word and journaled some thoughts, I put my pen down and waited. I was giving the Lord room to speak by just being still and quiet. The Lord responded by bringing a picture to my mind (actually it was more like a video).

In this picture, I was standing on stage in the church building where I pastor. I had my arm around a young man who'd recently put his trust in Jesus and I was asking the congregation, "Is there anyone here who could disciple this guy to a place where he could disciple someone else?" No one's hand went up.

I was thankful this was a spiritual picture and not reality, but I also felt an undeniable sense that this was indeed a picture of our church— no one (or not many) knew how to make a disciple who could make a disciple. In that moment I felt Jesus convicting me. He wasn't condemning me or shaking his head in disappointment, but I knew deep down he was saying, "Kirk, what you're doing isn't going to accomplish what I commanded in the Great Commission. I want you to make disciples who make disciples."

While this sounds like a calling I should have embraced *before* becoming a pastor—and truth be told, I thought I was making disciples—the reality is that I was

I was a groomsman who loved being in the middle of the aisle.

a groomsman who loved being in the middle of the aisle. I had an addiction to Sunday morning.

This isn't to say that our church wasn't invested in ministry efforts beyond Sunday morning. To the contrary, we regularly had over 20% of our adults engage in mission outreaches locally and globally every year…we had 87% of our Sunday attendance also engaged in a weekday Lifegroup…we had a financial goal of investing 30% of every dollar in missions outside of our church. Quite a few people thought we were knocking it out of the proverbial park.

I loved our staff and the great work they were doing, but as we'd grown in numbers and other ways, I realized my heart and my identity had become attached to Sunday morning. (Can you relate to that?)

To be completely honest, if you'd looked at the measuring scale of my heart, all the other things that were going "great" couldn't outweigh the worry or sense of inadequacy I felt if our Sunday gatherings weren't meeting my expectations. If more people weren't coming and we were not growing at the rate I "needed" to satiate my addiction, I struggled with feelings of failure. (Yikes! Who would want to follow a guy in that condition? I wouldn't.)

Subconsciously I believed that if I could just preach better—more clearly or more passionately—*then* people would want to take up their cross and follow Jesus. Thankfully, generous Jesus arrested my attention, "Kirk, your job is to make disciples who make disciples."

GOD'S SEVERE MERCY

In the vision I've just described, Jesus was expressing what I refer to as his severe mercy. I didn't want to see the vision Jesus showed me, but my soul desperately needed to see it. In his great mercy, he was sharing a hard truth with me because he loves his Bride too much to let her walk down a path that leads to less than his best.

Good parents do this with their dearly loved children all the time. We discipline or direct our children in ways that they prefer we didn't, but we do so because of our great love for them.

When Jesus expresses severe mercy it's almost always because something particularly big is on the line in terms of his plan for our lives. He doesn't always ring the bell of his mercy so loudly—sometimes he uses less intense communication—but when he does, there's always a reason.

As you read this, if you feel a twinge of conviction or if you feel like you just got gut-punched, don't run. Don't turn to something else to distract you from what Jesus is doing. Receiving the Lord's severe mercy always involves pain and joy. The pain is usually associated with the offense to our flesh combined with the undeniable realization that Jesus is absolutely right in whatever pronouncement he has made to us. This was certainly the case for me.

Had it been another person instead of Jesus who had confronted me with this conviction, I likely would have immediately sought to justify myself. My internal defense attorney would have stood up yelling,

"Objection!" I'd have responded by sharing about the effectiveness of our ministries and all the ways and efforts in which our church actually was making disciples. (I always have a ready list of accomplishments to pull out.) But this wasn't just another person sharing their opinion with me, this was Jesus—and I knew he was right.

Importantly, Jesus had communicated with me with crystal clarity, but also with gentleness. I felt deep conviction, but not a hint of condemnation from him. He wasn't angry nor was he against me—he was and is for me—but the Church is his bride, and he loves her and me too much to allow either one of us to walk down a futile path without redirecting us.

While it's true I wasn't crushed, I *was* undone. I was working hard. I had a busy schedule with every day filled with more objectives than I could accomplish. I was mobilizing lots of ministry resources all with the intent of making disciples, but Jesus had just told me I actually was not doing it, at least not in the way or to the degree he desired.

His words were hard for my flesh to hear, but I had to hear them. I felt the fire of the Holy Spirit's conviction, a fire that's not intended to torture, but one that is designed to purify and refine.

So what was I to do? How was I to respond? The right response to conviction is always to agree with Jesus (another way to describe repentance). Agreeing immediately takes you through the fire of conviction to where your soul can see Jesus smiling with arms open wide to reaffirm his love for you. When the Holy Spirit convicted me, I honestly had no idea in the moment how to "fix" the problem, but that wasn't the thing for which Jesus was looking. All he wanted was for me to agree with him. And so I did.

I literally said out loud, "Yes, Lord! You are right. I don't know what to do next, but I commit myself to making disciples who make disciples."

Apart from the convicting vision Jesus shared with me, I don't know that I would have had the courage or the insight to come to the conclusion that something needed to change in my approach to ministry.

Could I have done so on my own without his obvious intervention? I'm thinking not, hence the vision he gave me. What about you?

Is the Holy Spirit speaking anything to you right now through the personal stories I've just shared? Are you measuring the success of your ministry with a different metric than that of Jesus? Are you employing a different strategy than the one Jesus has already given us?

Take courage and ask him, "Is what I'm doing going to accomplish what you commanded?" Take 60 seconds right now to reflect and listen to his response.

PAUSE

If in your moment of reflection you experienced any kind of a sinking feeling, like "Oh no, I'm doing the same thing Kirk was doing." Don't despair. Don't let our spiritual enemy manipulate your perception of the Lord's conviction as he attempts to convert it to condemnation. If you're feeling conviction, it's because your heart is soft to Jesus' heart. He's knocking on the door of your heart about this because he has confidence you'll answer!

Reject condemnation and the enemy's lies about being a failure—Just say, "Yes!" to Jesus.

Literally out loud say, "Yes, Lord, I agree with you. I don't know what to do about it, but I'm not going to avoid your gaze. I'm not going to brush this conviction off or try to find some way to distract me from this uncomfortable feeling. You are right. I commit myself to making disciples who make disciples as you commanded."

JESUS IS A SLOPPY BLESSER

The moment you agree with Jesus, saying "Yes, Lord!" is the moment Jesus starts blessing. I mean it. When you say "Yes!" but before you have done anything else good or bad, Jesus starts blessing your "Yes!"—and he's a Sloppy Blesser. Let me explain...

Jesus is a Sloppy Blesser.

If I drew an 'X' on the floor and then opened a bottle of water and poured it on the 'X', the water would not only hit the mark, it would splatter all over the place. That's how Jesus blesses.

The moment we say "Yes!" to his admonition for disciple making (or anything else for that matter), Jesus blesses our response. Not only will our efforts in disciple making experience the supernatural advantage of the Holy Spirit's power, but so will other areas of our ministry and your life.

He might inject new joy into your marriage. He might create new unity in your staff. He might raise up volunteer leaders you'd never expected. He might begin to positively change your church's finances. I can't predict the splatter pattern of God's blessing in your life, but the principle of the Sloppy Blesser is a fact. God always enjoys doing more than we ask or imagine.[37]

The instant we commit ourselves to Jesus' strategy for building his Church through reproducible disciple making and before we've made any effort, he will begin to bless...and thanks be to God, he is a Sloppy Blesser.

---

37 Ephesians 3:20

CHAPTER 15

CREATING A DISCIPLE MAKING CULTURE IN THE AMERICAN CHURCH MODEL

As I began to search and read about how to create a disciple making culture, Jesus, in his generous way, exposed me to several people who were further down the path. Some were leading disciple making movements in China or India that were producing numbers and fruit that were unheard of in the U.S. I was amazed, humbled, and encouraged all at the same time. However, I struggled with how to assimilate their approach into my context—the prevailing American Church model.[38]

For our sake, I'll define this model as one with a building or campus that is considered by members as the primary gathering place of the church. In the American Church model there's a paid staff leading various common ministries and any Sunday morning gatherings are peak events in terms of time, resources, and attendance.

Most of the books I was reading were about disciple making movements that were taking place in rural, poorer contexts where the scope of daily life activities occurred in a much smaller geographic domain and where the societal culture was far more relational than ours.

---

38 Sometimes referred to as the Legacy Church model.

Other disciple making movements were occurring in dense urban centers rather than in the suburban, middle to upper-middle-class communities like our environment. These were not and are not excuses, they are real variables that must be considered.

How can I create a reproducible disciple making culture in an American Church model?

The question facing me was: How can I create a reproducible disciple making culture in an American Church model?

Do I have to resign from my position and start roaming the local coffee shops looking for the spiritually hungry? I'd had a friend who'd planted around the same time as me who'd done exactly this. Was Jesus asking me to do that? What about all the people I'd be leaving behind? I'd started this church in an elementary school 20 years ago. My fingerprints were everywhere. This isn't a boastful comment, it simply expresses the sense of responsibility I felt. I'd led us to where we were presently; I had to stay and help lead us to where Jesus was calling.

Additionally, 99% of churches in our country are presently operating within the prevailing American Church model. These churches represent billions of dollars of kingdom resources and millions of people—and they will continue for generations to come. It's not realistic to expect millions of people and hundreds of thousands of pastors to abandon the church culture that shaped them. My point is that while the present American Church model may change one day, it's going to happen incrementally, not in one fell swoop. The most logical approach is to work toward creating a disciple making culture within the American Church model, to bend it to a disciple making vision.

BUT WHERE TO BEGIN?

My first step toward answering this question was initially disheartening but then dramatically transforming.

A friend of mine, Brad Sprague, introduced me to David Broodryk, a sort of disciple making influencer.[39] In my first meeting with David, he asked our team to consider what I thought was a crazy question:

If you were going to start a church in a way that was opposite of the Great Commission, what would it look like?[40]

On the surface, his proposal sounded preposterous and I told him so, but David asked me to humor him and so I did. Together my team and I examined each phrase of the Great Commission. It didn't take long before I began to feel uncomfortable. Boiled down, our findings could be summarized like this:

THE GREAT COMMISSION	OPPOSITE THE GREAT COMMISSION
All authority has been given to me (Jesus)	All authority would vest with me (the pastor or leaders)
Go and make disciples of all nations	Come, attend, listen
Baptizing them in my name	Emphasizing church membership or volunteering

---

39 David Broodryk is the founder of Two Four Eight which seeks to multiply disciple making movements in the cities of the world. https://twofoureight.org.
40 Matthew 18:18–20

Teaching them to obey all that I have commanded you	Teaching them to consider embracing whatever seems relevant. Leave the disciple making to pastors, sermons, youth groups, etc.

As we were engaged in this exercise, I began to see more clearly and concretely what Jesus had meant when he said, "Kirk, what you're doing isn't going to accomplish what I commanded in the Great Commission."

The exercise helped me identify places where I was doing ministry that, at the very least, were not in sync with Jesus' strategy. I was only partially comforted by the fact that I wasn't alone in this realization. Our whole team identified ways in which they were doing the same thing.

While this was initially disheartening, with David facilitating, we began to realize that if we could identify actual ways in which we were doing ministry opposite to the Great Commission, then we could surely find ways to execute these ministries differently, which meant there was hope!

What I'll be sharing in the next chapters is how we changed—and are changing—the culture of our church into one of disciple making.

Over the last few years, I've worked closely with over 100 pastors, meeting weekly with them for between 2–9 months each, as we seek together to create a sustainable, effective disciple making culture in our churches. Here's what I've discovered: It's hard.

Part of what makes it hard is that every one of these pastors, including me—and likely you or your pastor—grew up in a culture where disciple making was more or less the goal of a particular ministry department within the church.

Disciple making was expressed as a course, a class, a workbook, an expository Bible study, or whatever, but reproducible disciple making

Disciple making was expressed as a course, a class, a workbook, an expository Bible study, or whatever, but reproducible disciple making never defined the culture of the church.

never defined the culture of the church. A consistent, clear disciple making vision didn't permeate every single context of the church. There wasn't consistent language, unified strategy, or accessible steps that people encountered in each context that wove threads of disciple making through the *whole* church, in every person, and in every household.

Previously if the efforts of our staff had been depicted as a team of oxen, I would describe us all as plowing diligently…but we were all headed in our own direction, plowing our own field.

Think about it…does that describe your experience?

CHAPTER 16

THREADS OF DISCIPLE MAKING

"DISCIPLE MAKING ISN'T AN EMPHASIS OF A MINISTRY DEPARTMENT WITHIN A CHURCH, IT IS THE ENTIRETY OF THE CHURCH'S MISSION."

I would respectfully assert that the prevailing church culture in America is not actually a reproducible disciple making culture. It wants to be, but it isn't. I thought I had a disciple making culture, but as I've shared, despite the good things we were doing and the wonderful fruit we saw, there was so much more Jesus had and still has for us.

Part of the problem was my default setting. I was "doing" church as I'd seen it done in every church of which I'd been a part—even as I'd learned it in seminary. But now, I'm convinced that in spite of all that doing, it isn't working. Do you sense this?

If we had a disciple making culture, then Lifeway wouldn't have published research showing that two-thirds of children who grow up in evangelical churches for at least part of their childhood wind up leaving the church for at least a year or more after high school; a pivotal year from which many don't return.[41]

If we had a genuine disciple making culture, then we wouldn't be spending on average 91% of the American Church's resources on Christians instead of reaching the lost both locally and globally.

My friend David Broodryk shared a chart with me showing the results of a massive survey conducted by The Center for The Study of Global Christianity, taken by millions of Christians. It showed that the longer people are Christians and church members, the weaker their spirituality, commitment, and eagerness to grow becomes. Can you imagine living in a marriage like that? With every anniversary the relationship is less in every way than the year before. Yuck!

How could we all be working so hard to make disciples and still see statistics like this?

It's a problem of not seeing the forest for the trees. Pastors and leaders in American churches have been doing church in much the same way for a long time. Even when we start new churches, we structure them like they've "always" been structured. We make discipleship a program or a class or a department. We don't weave consistent, recognizable disciple making themes into the fabric of the church.

THE WARP AND WOOF OF IT

Weaving is an apt metaphor here. There are lots of different methods of weaving. Across the different methods and despite how technology has sped up the process, weaving remains essentially the same, and it's mesmerizing to watch.

When weaving on a loom, a device called a shuttle is loaded with

---

41 In case you missed this link the first time I mentioned it...Lifeway Research. "Reasons 18- to 22-Year-Olds Drop Out of Church." Accessed September 4, 2024. https://research.lifeway.com/2007/08/07/reasons-18-to-22-year-olds-drop-out-of-church.

thread and repeatedly pushed horizontally from one side and then back again creating what's referred to as the woof (or weft). The shuttle, with its line of thread trailing, is pushed by the weaver and glides horizontally across vertical threads called the warp which are raised or lowered so that the shuttle goes above some and below others, creating a pattern in the rug or fabric.

When the shuttle has carried its thread from one side to another, the weaver uses a beater or batten to press the thread down tightly.[42]

Here's what I'm getting at…If the shuttle carries a blue thread, then that blue thread will show up all the way across the fabric. Again, it may go in front or behind the longitudinal threads, but it's woven into the entire fabric.

Disciple making is supposed to be like this. It's not an emphasis of a particular department of the church. Disciple making is the entirety of the mission of the church. The goal—Jesus' strategy—-is for us to weave the threads of disciple making into the whole fabric of the church.

At the risk of mixing metaphors, there's a bit of "new wineskin" thinking that applies. In my disciple making journey, I had to unlearn some things that inadvertently undermined our efforts to create a disciple making culture in our church. I'm betting you will too. It will feel awkward and you might be tempted to bail, but don't. It's worth it, I promise.

BE PATIENT JUST A LITTLE LONGER

The practical stuff is coming—really it is—but I want you to resist a little longer jumping to that portion of the book.

More than once I've had pastor friends ask me for our disciple making "stuff." I used to comply with these requests, but not once—and

---

42 Here's a 30-second video that will give you a visual: TinyUrl.com/bddad2ar.

I'm not exaggerating—not once did any of those pastors see the dream of a disciple making culture realized in their church. Instead, they worked really hard only to see it not catch on and so they moved on to the "next" thing, just like I used to do.

It wasn't because of a lack of commitment or good intentions, it's because there are some underlying principles so ingrained in how we've learned to do church that we don't easily recognize the undermining effect they have.

Remember, weaving is tedious. Handcrafted rugs or fabrics require time. One of the most significant traits required of the best weavers who weave the most beautiful and highest quality of rugs is persistence. Staying after it...not giving up.

One of the most common statements I make when talking with pastors/leaders about disciple making is this: I'm no expert in disciple making, but I'm unswervingly committed. I'm not giving up. I'm done thinking a 6-week series will "do the trick." I'm finished trying to apply a method or a curriculum as the answer to the challenge.

Our team and I are simply not going to give up asking the question: Are we making disciples who make disciples?

Instead, I'm going to look at everything in our church, from my staff meeting, to our budget, to our ministry contexts, and everything else to make sure that we're consistently weaving threads of disciple making into all of them. Our team and I are simply not going to give up asking the question: Are we making disciples who make disciples?

It's our only metric.

CHAPTER 17

FOUR PRINCIPLES FOR CREATING CULTURE

"CHANGING CULTURE IS LIKE WEAVING—IT'S INTENTIONAL AND TAKES PERSISTENCE."

More and more pastors are feeling a fire being kindled in their hearts for reproducible disciple making—maybe you're one of these (I hope so!). In my experience, pastors respond to this new fire in one of these four ways:

1. THEY ATTEMPT TO ROLL OUT DISCIPLESHIP PROGRAMS TO ADD TO THEIR AMERICAN CHURCH MODEL

Often this materializes as a training course with modules of various content, received with great excitement among those already wanting more of this content. Those attending these courses almost always grow, but the impact is limited to this subculture and doesn't often change the broader culture of the church. It's often curriculum-based and therefore not easily reproduced. Even more important though, these courses are added on top of an American church model still consuming most of the staff attention and the church's resources. While a disciple making track is important, I believe it's only a piece of a bigger puzzle.

129

2. THEY LAUNCH A DISCIPLESHIP GROUP MINISTRY

This is where I started. After some false starts, I got into a groove of discipling 2-3 guys using the Core Experiences and Starting Points I've described in this book. This was so life giving! We saw men confronting sin...men obeying God's Word...men learning to hear the Lord and share their faith...and lots of others things. The problem? Our church was still investing millions of dollars operating all the ministries common to the prevailing American model of church. Expecting D Groups to change the church culture was like expecting the tail to wag the dog.

3. THEY GIVE UP

The saddest outcome I see is when a pastor thinks that a sermon series on disciple making or a 12-week course is going to "do the trick." They roll out a program or seasonal emphasis, but find that the congregation—and the staff—are still operating under an old paradigm. As Peter Drucker or Mark Fields have said, "Culture eats strategy for lunch." When this strategy doesn't produce the disciple making culture a pastor is hoping for, they often return to business as usual. After all, the seven day cycle of American church can keep a pastor busy for their entire vocational lives. (Yuck! Who wants to settle for that?!)

4. THEY CREATE A NEW CULTURE BY LEVERAGING EVERY MINISTRY CONTEXT FOR ITS DISCIPLE MAKING POTENTIAL

A growing number of churches are finding ways to weave disciple making into the American church model. They aren't dumping the model, they're bending every ministry context to serve Jesus' Great Commandment. They're learning to weave threads of reproducible disciple making into everything—and it's working!

While it takes a few years to change the culture of an organization, if you choose this path, you'll find that encouraging results emerge almost immediately. You'll see life transformation and you'll know you're on the right track. Let's explore what that can look like in the church you help lead...

How to Change the Culture of an Organization

My trip to the New Mexico Pueblo as a child didn't teach me much about weaving, but I picked up on this one thing: If you're weaving a blue rug, you need to weave in blue threads through the whole thing. Similarly, if you want a disciple making culture in your church, you need to weave threads of disciple making into every part of it.

Here are four basic principles for creating culture in any organization.[43] Our training provides coaching for this process. We're going to apply them to disciple making within the church, but they are applicable for any organization. If you want to create a specific culture you need to:

1. IDENTIFY YOUR PREFERRED OUTCOME

In our church we say:

> We want to learn to enjoy and follow Jesus together
> in a way we can show others how to enjoy and follow him too.

This is the outcome we desire for everyone in our church. Everything we do aims for this target. We plan and measure everything we do with this outcome in mind.

---

43 We offer coaching plans to help your team through this process. See the last page of the book for more on this.

You don't have to use my language—use your own—but you must be able to state your preferred outcome in a way that fits your church and in a way that you and your leaders can and will repeat.

To show you how simple yet powerful this concept is, let's use a non-sensical example...Imagine that your preferred outcome was for everyone to aspire to be an accomplished gymnast. You want them to do back hand springs and flips and twists and you want them to be able to show others how to do them too. You know they won't all progress at the same rate or reach the same level of competency, but if you want them to progress at all, you must identify your preferred outcome. Which leads us to our second principle for creating culture in an organization...

2. IDENTIFY THE SIMPLEST, MOST REPRODUCIBLE EXPRESSIONS OF YOUR PREFERRED OUTCOME

These are the threads you're going to weave into every ministry context in your church. These expressions of your outcome are what you want everyone to catch. If they do, you're counting on them wanting more and going for more. Do they need more than these most simple, reproducible expressions? Of course, and you should always have "next steps," but you can't create a culture if you skip this step.

Returning to our gymnastics illustration...What might you consider the simplest most reproducible expressions of being a gymnast? Likely choices would include a forward roll, a backward roll, stand on your head, and a cartwheel.

Does a person need more than these four to be an accomplished gymnast? Absolutely, but mastering these four lets them experience the joy of gymnastics, and gives them confidence, and a sense of expectancy regarding what's to come. These four skills are starting points.

In the language of the church I help pastor, we've identified the four Core Experiences discussed in chapters 7-10. We believe—and years of experience supports our belief— that if people learn a simple way of studying the Bible (DBS), and if we can show (not just tell) them how to encounter Jesus in these four ways, then their enjoyment of Jesus will spur them on to greater and deeper ways of enjoying and following him.

3. RELENTLESSLY MODEL THESE REPRODUCIBLE EXPRESSIONS WITH COMMON LANGUAGE AND COMMON PRACTICES IN EVERY CONTEXT WITHIN YOUR ORGANIZATION

Every ministry context in a church is unique in various ways from the others, but each provides an opportunity to model the simple expressions of your preferred outcome.

If becoming an accomplished gymnast was our preferred outcome, on Sundays I would not only teach about it, I'd also model it, and even make room for the congregation to try it too. You can bet the kids would be doing it in KidZone and the teens would be doing it in our student ministry.

I'm intentionally not using the phrasing and language of my church because I'm guessing you already have language. I don't want you to feel pressure to adopt ours. Whatever reproducible expressions of disciple making you settle on, if you are relentless in modeling them, the aroma of disciple making will be easily detectable to anyone who spends at least a few weeks in your church. (We'll cover more practicals on this important principle in a minute.)

It's at this point where the Three Values of Disciple Making I mentioned in Chapter 4 become vitally important. Even though you've identified your preferred outcome and the reproducible expressions of it, when leaders begin to actually model it, they will struggle against the inevitable creep of their default paradigm. Remember, these leaders (and you, for that matter) have been "doing church" a certain way for years in some cases. The urge to be a groomsman or bridesmaid in the aisle will be hard to resist. Re-read Chapter 4 now that you've come this far and you'll see better how the Three Values of Disciple Making will help you and your leaders train each other and evaluate your progress.

4. SHARE THE STORIES OF SUCCESS, BOTH BIG AND SMALL

Ordinary people sharing how they are enjoying and following our extraordinary Jesus is compelling and convincing. It's essential for creating a culture of disciple making.

Every time I hear anything that sounds even vaguely like a success story, I jump on it. The power of testimony can't be overstated. If someone has a story of God's answering the Include Me prayer, I want to help them share it with as many people as I can. If someone had the opportunity to ask the Miracle Question of a coworker during the week, I'll shorten my sermon to make room for this story of someone living out our preferred outcome.

The rest of this book is about how to implement these four principles and what it might actually look like. Keep reading and you'll see a pathway for weaving disciple making into every context of your church and changing the culture forever.

CHAPTER 18

CIRCLES NOT SILOS

If you want a disciple making culture in your church, you need to weave threads of disciple making into every part of it. Here's a way to go about it...

We're all familiar with org charts that show who reports to whom and in what areas. Similar to that, I want you to create a chart that shows every one of the relational contexts of your church based upon the size of the group. We categorize them by size because the number of people involved in a group is the key variable to the relational dynamic. The goal is to identify every single ministry in the church. It represents everything over which you and your team have been given stewardship.

Use the three darker circles in the example on the next page as your main categories and then draw circles below them that reflect every ministry context of your church based upon the size of the gathering. Use your own terms and feel free to add/subtract circles, just make sure every relational context is represented. Don't forget ministry experiences like retreats or mission outreaches; while they are short term, we include them because they are contexts in which the Core Experiences can be woven. Here's a simple example of what this chart might look like:

Relational Contexts of the Church

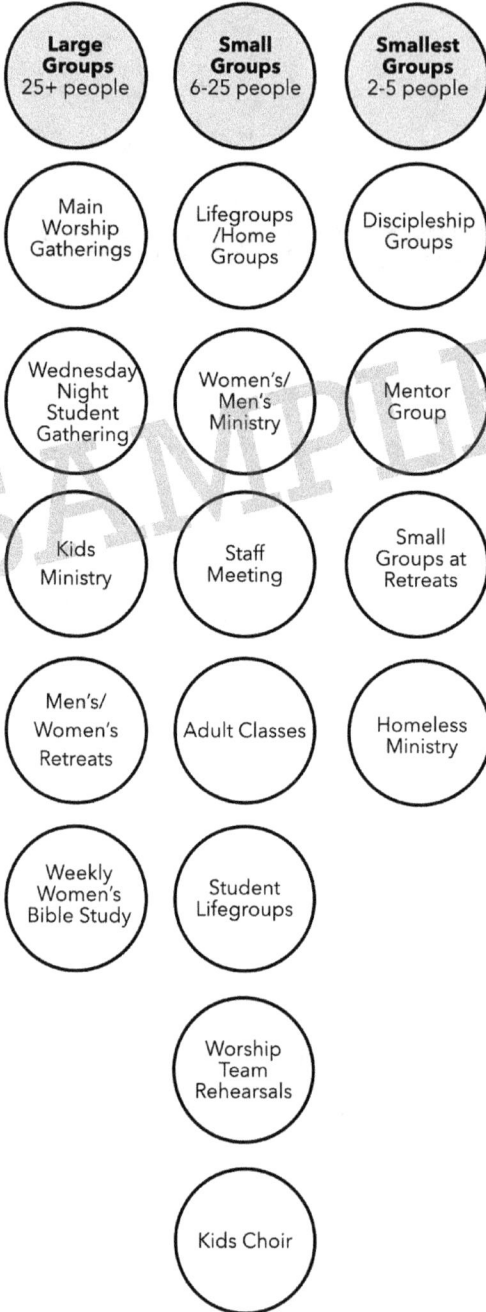

Large Groups 25+ people	Small Groups 6-25 people	Smallest Groups 2-5 people
Main Worship Gatherings	Lifegroups /Home Groups	Discipleship Groups
Wednesday Night Student Gathering	Women's/ Men's Ministry	Mentor Group
Kids Ministry	Staff Meeting	Small Groups at Retreats
Men's/ Women's Retreats	Adult Classes	Homeless Ministry
Weekly Women's Bible Study	Student Lifegroups	
	Worship Team Rehearsals	
	Kids Choir	

When our staff created a picture of our own ministry contexts, we were surprised by just how many relational circles we were stewarding. We had way more circles than anyone would have expected! As we examined each, we recognized that there was something genuinely good happening in every circle. Hopefully you feel that way too. But I was blind to the potential each circle had to be better than good—they could be great.

For many years, each of these relational circles of ministry functioned like a silo. While our entire staff team all embraced the vision statement describing our preferred outcome, that was where any synergy ended. Each team member employed their own strategy for reaching that outcome. We functioned as independent silos…but not anymore. After relentlessly weaving in the simplest expressions of our preferred outcome into each context using common language and common practices, the culture of disciple making is now almost immediately detectable in each.

ASSESSING THE POTENTIAL OF EACH CIRCLE

Let's explore the two-step process for beginning to weave disciple making into every context of your own church:

1. Assess the strength and limitations of each circle of ministry.
2. Determine how to leverage the strength of each circle to model the simplest, most reproducible experiences of our preferred outcome.

Each ministry context brings something unique to the table. Identifying these distinctive strengths will help you leverage their potential and also help you set realistic expectations.

Main Worship Gatherings

Strengths

Spiritual Authority
Largest Gathering
Modeling Vision

In the Large Group category, let's consider your Main Sunday Service(s). Two of the strengths of this context is that it's led by the person of greatest spiritual authority in the church and has the largest number of people present. These make it ideal for affirming vision and for modeling what we're after. On the flip side, it's weak on accountability. We may preach and even model what we're after, but we generally have no idea if obedience follows.

Lifegroups

Strengths

Intimacy
Reproducible
Good First Step
Whole Household

In contrast, one of the ministries that takes place in our Small Groups is our home-based Lifegroup. These small groups "score" stronger in other ways. Our Lifegroups involve the whole family—parents and kids. In fact it's the only regular time in our church when whole households gather together instead of being segregated by life stage. These groups are much more intimate than our Sunday services and a great first step for experiencing the Starting Points of our Core Experiences.

Disciplemaking Groups

Strengths

Accountability
Intimacy
Activation
Reproducible

In the Smallest Group category, consider the strengths of the D-group context. It's the best for accountability and for actually activating our faith in the world. It's reproducible and life-giving.

I could go through the other circles of ministry contexts and I could have identified the weaknesses of each circle, but I'm sure you see where I'm going.

Every ministry context, including staff meetings and training events, have strengths distinctive to that context. The goal in this step is to identify these strengths so we can leverage those strengths for their disciple making potential. When you complete the exercise of assessing what each circle brings to the party, you're ready for the second step…

KNOCKING DOWN THE SILOS

The second step is where we look at each ministry context and each of the Core Experiences and Starting Points, brainstorming together, "How can we weave these into our Sunday services…our KidZone classes… our Student Lifegroups…our staff meeting, etc.?" (Don't forget the goal: To leverage all of the strengths of all of the contexts for their disciple making potential.)

Leverage all of the strengths of all of the contexts for their disciple making potential.

This exercise is like a group working on a jigsaw puzzle. I openly admit that I despise jigsaw puzzles, but putting this one together was invigorating. Each time we moved to a new relational context, thinking together what it might look like to model one of the Core Experiences, the mental wheels would begin to turn and something good would emerge. It was like putting together a jigsaw puzzle of a treasure map—that led to real treasure!

Recently I was at our student ministry's Beach Week. It involves hundreds of students heading to the beach, complete with ocean, jellyfish, and sharks…what could possibly go wrong?! I attended only as an observer and to high-five students; I had absolutely zero input on the planning of our activities or teaching sessions. They didn't even invite me to preach.

At the week long event, I was blown away as different volunteer leaders came on stage and each one spoke our common language of disciple making. Our students were learning the Include Me prayer and the Miracle Question...and going out on the beach to pray for others. I forget what the theme of each evening messages was, but I remember clearly that the teachers included times of Listening to the Lord.
Our student ministry staff were modeling the Core Experiences with common language and common practice. This didn't happen overnight. Please remember, changing the culture of a church requires relentless commitment over the years...but it works...and it works predictably because it's based on the values Jesus expressed in the Great Commission and Great Commandment.

I know I'm just hitting the high points here of a more detailed process of assessing your entire church's ministry, but I'm betting that you can see the simplicity of the process. You can do this, and when you do, your staff team will be on the same page like never before.[44]

TO WHAT END?

Before I show you what it actually looks like to weave the Core Experiences into every relational context, it's important that we zoom out for a moment to see the big picture. Why are we doing all this work? Is it to have a healthy church?...Is it to connect everyone in a disciple making relationship?...To advance toward spiritual maturity? The answer, of course, is "yes" but there's more to it.

God's ultimate goal is for knowledge of his glory to so permeate the world—influencing everyone and everything—that he likens it to

---

44 In Chapter 21 I share about training events and cohorts we offer to help you through this process.

covering the earth like the waters cover the sea.[45] His presence, priorities, power, and personality will saturate everything! When this happens, he says that everything in heaven and earth will come into perfect unity under the authority of Jesus.[46] All God's dreams come true! No wonder the Spirit and the bride say, "Come!"[47]

If that weren't enough, in his immense generosity, Jesus is including his people in the process. Again, this isn't a "have to" kind of thing, it's a "get to" kind of thing. He literally wants to share his glory with us.[48] And, He wants his good news to reach every person in every nation on earth.[49] This is God's endgame. The question is: Does our endgame match God's?

If growing our church is our goal, we'll never reach our city or the world with the gospel. Conversely, if we align our hearts with God's—to bring his sweet good news into our homes, workplaces, cities and the nations—we can trust God to grow our churches. I readily admit, that initially I was scared to death to release my grip on the priority of growing our church. Ultimately, though, I aligned my heart and my strategy with God's and found this principle to be wonderfully true.

Why am I spending so much time emphasizing this point? Because if the senior leaders of a church are not convinced of God's ultimate goal of our making disciples of all nations for the sake of his glory, then the fruit of our "discipleship" efforts will never spread beyond the church walls. We may find that we have given our lives for the sake of the seven day cycle of American Church. Never, Lord! Instead, let's be leaders who walk closely in the footsteps of Jesus.

The graphic on the following page helps me connect all that our team is doing in the local church to God's endgame:

---

45 Habakkuk 2:14
46 Ephesians 1:9-10
47 Revelation 22:17
48 Romans 8:17; 2 Thessalonians 2:18
49 Matthew 28:18-20

We Steward the Relational Contexts of the Church to…

SAMPLE

Large Groups
25+ people

Main Worship Gatherings

Kids Ministry

Wednesday Night Student Gathering

Men's/ Women's Retreats

Weekly Women's/ Women's Bible Study

Small Groups
6-25 people

Lifegroups /Home Groups

Women's/ Men's Ministry

Staff Meeting

Adult Classes

Student Lifegroups

Worship Team Rehearsals

Kids Choir

Smallest Groups
2-5 people

Discipleship Groups

Mentor Group

Small Groups at Retreats

Homeless Ministry

Show the Church How to Enjoy and Follow Jesus Together…

Individual

Marriage

Family

Church Family

To Show Others How to Enjoy and Follow Him too!

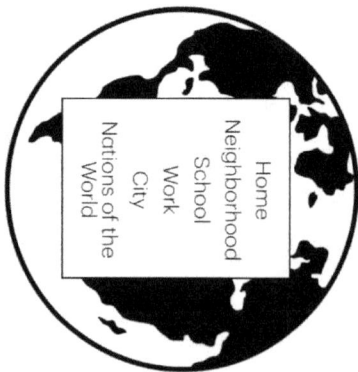

Home
Neighborhood
School
Work
City
Nations of the World

142

If all of this seems exciting yet overwhelming at the same time, let me remind you of the amazing spiritual principle I shared in Chapter 14:

The moment you align your heart with God's priority is the moment God begins to bless.

The moment you align your heart with God's priority is the moment God begins to bless. The moment you commit your heart to cultivating a disciple making culture in your church, you will begin to find hard things becoming easier. It's sort of like jumping into a flowing river—the moment you do, you begin to move—even before you start swimming.

Now, let me show you what it might look like actually to weave the Core Experiences into each circle.

CHAPTER 19

WEAVING IN THE CORE EXPERIENCES

You may not be the lead pastor, but pretend for a moment that you just preached the sermon on Sunday morning in your church.

You studied the Word the week before. You made sure your heart was in step with Jesus. You honed your outline, sharpened your illustrations, and then you shared it with genuine passion with those who attended.

What happens next? An invitation? A ministry time? Thanks for coming, that's all for now?

What if at the end of the sermon you gave just a little room for people to personally encounter the Jesus you just told them about?

What if, like a faithful groomsman, you moved to the side giving them the chance to have an unobstructed view of Jesus? Here's what that could look like…

#1 Weaving in Listening to the Lord

MAIN WORSHIP GATHERINGS

It's not hard to weave the thread of Listening to the Lord into your church's Sunday gathering. Here's a way I often do it...

Everyone receives a card and golf pencil when they enter our auditorium. I leave five minutes (sometimes ten) at the end of my sermon for a listening time.[50] I reference John 10:27 and that Jesus wants to speak personally to us, and remind them of the simple ways we can test and approve what we sense is from the Lord (Chapter 7). Then, using the "I want you to know..." Starting Point, we listen to the Lord.

When we do this with our church, we have the sound guy play an ambient music track. Then we give people about two minutes of uninterrupted time to let Jesus complete the sentence.

I admit I was nervous the first time I did this. Plus I was a little concerned about those who were streaming the service online. Would they tune out? I decided it didn't matter, not compared to leading people to experience Jesus.

If I do nothing more than what I've just described, then I count it as a success. Sometimes though, I take it one step further. After we've listened and written down what we've sensed from the Lord, I'll invite any of our elders, Lifegroup leaders, or ministry team leaders to stand and share what they heard from the Lord.

The first time I did this, I was scared—what if no one stood up? But they did...and they do...every time. People share profoundly, deeply, and

---

50 When I first considered doing this, I was concerned about how to find time to squeeze this into our already full order of service, but then I was reminded that our goal is to be a groomsmen and bridesmaids to the side of the aisle. What could be more important than using my influence to let people encounter the groom?

genuinely what the Lord said to them. And it's always powerful. It gives our church the chance to hear different ways the Lord speaks personally to his children. Because I limit the scope of who can share to those who are in leadership, I don't have to worry about someone saying something wacky.

Why is it important to do this in the context of our Sunday gatherings? This is the context where the most people gather. It's where the person(s) with the most authority in the church generally speak. It's where the vision and direction for the church are espoused and explained. When we weave the thread of Listening to the Lord into this circle, it sets the direction for the whole church. When I take time to weave in this thread or any other, everyone immediately knows: This is important.

I can't measure the impact of weaving in this thread, but because the threads of disciple making are being woven concurrently in every circle, our prioritizing it on Sunday establishes and validates it very effectively.

CHILDREN'S MINISTRY

In your children's classes on Sunday mornings, regardless of what curriculum your team uses, leave 5-10 minutes at the end to share with the kids that: "God is the best Father in the whole world and just like every good daddy, he loves to talk with his children. We're going to close our eyes and listen to see if he wants to say anything to us right now. Usually, he reminds us of how much he loves us and how good he is. Let's listen now."

After a short moment, ask the kids if the Lord said anything to anyone. It's easy to affirm or gently correct what's shared.

STUDENT MINISTRY

If you have teaching time which leads to a small group discussion, end the discussion by using the Starting Points to teach the students to listen to the Lord and to share with one another. This has transformed our Student Ministry.

SMALL GROUPS

Each week at some point in the Lifegroup we break into small groups of three to four men/women. We do a DBS and then practice one of the Core Experiences. Listening to the Lord is the most popular. Using the Core Experiences takes a load off the leader of the Lifegroup in terms of planning the meeting.

Our Lifegroup flow is simple and reproducible:

- Fellowship: usually a meal and time for catching up.
- Vision: we read Acts 2:42-47 and do hand motions with the kids.
- Announcements: someone simply pulls two relevant announcements from our website and shares the info with the group.
- Worship: We generally use YouTube videos, starting with a kid-friendly song.
- Core: We do a DBS and then one of the Core Experiences (After worship, kids exit for their own time led by a rotating parent, an older sibling, or a paid sitter.)

Once the five parts of the flow have been modeled, each can be assigned to different members of the Lifegroup to lead the following week so that no one person carries the weight of the group. Even better, when Lifegroup is led in this manner, we are leaving footprints behind so that everyone knows how to contribute to the group. This simple strategy makes multiplying groups so much easier.

The Flow isn't intended to be rigid. Even though our Lifegroups generally make it all the way through the Flow when they meet, that's not the point. We know that the Holy Spirit loves each aspect of the Flow and, if he chooses to emphasize one aspect on a given night, we want to be sensitive to that and enjoy what he's doing. Even in a Sunday school class, you can leave time at the end for Listening to the Lord. There's almost no context where this isn't possible.

DISCIPLESHIP GROUPS

Chapter 13 describes the C.A.L.L. format so I won't repeat it here. When we are practicing listening to the Lord, as part of the Learn It portion of our time, we do a DBS followed by a time of listening and journaling what we hear, using the "I want you to know…" Starting Point.

It's important to share with one another what we heard from the Lord, so we generally read journals out loud. This provides the opportunity to affirm or correct what a person received. It also helps break down the walls that the enemy tries to construct to make our faith something we just keep inside.

In each of the Core Experiences, including Listening to the Lord, it's valuable to then reflect and write down an "I will…" statement, which we also share with one another so we can celebrate our experience with Jesus when we next meet.

STAFF MEETING

As surprising as it may sound, making room for the Core Experiences is critical to the creation of a disciple making culture. The staff of a church is comprised of the key torch-bearers of the church's vision. I failed miserably when I tried to get my team on board simply by explaining the Core Experiences. Everything changed when I stopped *telling* and started *showing*.

Each week a portion of our staff meeting is devoted to experiencing Jesus. This serves a training function but also creates unity and friendship within the team.

FAMILY

We believe parents are the chief disciple makers of their children. We train them in simple ways to show their children how to experience Jesus. Every Starting Point I have mentioned can be introduced and shared within the family. Imagine how encouraging it is to see your own family as a Discipleship Group who organically disciples one another in the Core Experiences at bedtime with little ones, in conversations at the dinner table, and later in drive time. Being on mission becomes not just a summer trip but a way of life as you enjoy and follow Jesus together. When these Core Experiences are the foundation of your relationship with Jesus the soil for healthy families is cultivated daily.

#2 Weaving in Talking with the Lord

MAIN WORSHIP GATHERINGS

After concluding your sermon, you can briefly summarize Discovery Prayer and then do it together using the main Scripture from the sermon.

When I do this, I briefly model thanking the Lord for what the

Scripture reveals about him, then I give them time to pray themselves or write down things for which they can thank him.

I do the same with what the Scripture reveals about people. I model it by praying a short prayer that includes Declaring and/or Asking. Then I give them time to do these same things privately. I end by challenging them to talk with the Lord in this way and to do this in the coming week.

While the main Sunday gatherings don't provide much in terms of personal coaching, they go a long way in validating the truth that Jesus wants to talk with us. This will make the job of your Lifegroup leaders much easier.

As you and your team begin to think more about weaving in threads of disciple making, you'll no doubt come up with all sorts of creative ways to do it. I'm only sharing a few to show you how easy and natural it can be.

CHILDREN'S MINISTRY AND THE FAMILY

While younger ones might not be able to read a Scripture yet, it's easy to have each one thank God for something based upon that day's lesson. Children can learn to declare attributes of God together,

> "God you are mighty and strong!"
> "Jesus you love me and hear my prayers."
> "God you created the whole world and you made me
> just how you wanted me to be."

Older children can practice declaring to God who they saw him to be in the Bible story that day. They can also be taught a children's version of the Lord's Prayer and shown how to pray it in a way that is personally meaningful. This Scripture is one of the easiest models for Discovery Prayer and it lays a foundation for talking to God that Jesus first taught his disciples. Parents:

this is also a sweet practice that's easy to incorporate into the bedtime routine too!

Remember, a child that grows up in a church that's weaving in threads of disciple making is going to experience Jesus in every context. It's a great church in which to raise a family!

STUDENT MINISTRY

We practice Discovery Prayer in our student Lifegroups similar to what I describe below.

SMALL GROUPS

During what we refer to as the Core time, we break into smaller groups of three to four men/women. In a group of this size, even the most quiet person generally feels comfortable or at least compelled to participate.

We select a passage of Scripture—often from the most recent sermon, but not always. After sharing a DBS together, we pray together using Discovery Prayer. Starting with a DBS helps to reveal the very things for which we then Thank-Declare-Ask for in prayer.

When we pray together, we don't go "around the circle," but I do encourage each person in my breakout group to pray out loud. They usually do. It may be a very simple prayer straight out of the DBS we did a few minutes before, but there's always power in praying the Word of God.

Don't worry if your first attempt at this isn't as smooth in execution as you'd hoped. Remember, you're weaving and weaving takes time— stay at it. Success doesn't depend upon your perfect execution, it depends upon Jesus encountering people. He will.

DISCIPLESHIP GROUPS

We practice Discovery Prayer during the Learn It time. In this context, there's more time to debrief and more time in next week's meeting to share how our personal experience went during the week as we talked with the Lord.

STAFF MEETING

Once the staff has experienced talking with the Lord together a few times, it's simple to break them into groups to pray through a scripture, interceding for each other and the church. Prayer is so much deeper when we're confident we're praying in alignment with the heart of Jesus.

#3 Weaving in Listening to the Lord for Loving Others

MAIN WORSHIP GATHERINGS

A simple way to weave in this disciple making thread at the end of the sermon is to have people be still for one minute, asking Jesus to give them the name of a person he wants them to love, encourage, or with whom they need to reconcile.

It's genuinely amazing what Jesus says sometimes and just as amazing how people respond in obedience to him.

Once, the week we'd woven this experience into our Sunday gathering, a man pulled me aside and shared how he'd felt the Lord tell him to reconcile with his brother. He explained that since his father had died years before, his brother had distanced himself from their siblings and said hurtful things as he pushed them away. The man went on to explain that as a result of his brother's actions the burden of caring for their mother had fallen solely on him. He'd struggled with bitterness and unforgiveness toward his brother ever since…until he heard Jesus tell him to reach out to his brother in an attempt to reconcile. He was so convicted by the words of Jesus that he reached out to his brother. There's more to the story of course, but here's the point: When people hear Jesus, everything changes. When people hear Jesus and can test and approve his will as God promises in Romans 12:2, they are willing to do brave things—sacrificial and humble things—all in response to Jesus.

STUDENT MINISTRY

This experience has been woven into the culture of our student ministry to great effect. Often during student worship times at our weekly student gathering or on retreats, our leadership team will encourage students to See-Feel-Respond during the worship time or in small groups, giving God room to lead them to encourage or pray for someone in the room or group.

Where this is new, a simple exercise that fosters the idea of encouragement is a good place to begin, such as giving each student a card with the name of another student in the group. They then ask the Lord for a word or verse to share as an encouragement.

CHILDREN'S MINISTRY AND THE FAMILY

We give our children time to ask the Lord to remind them of someone to whom they might say "I love you." Sometimes we lead the children to ask God, "Who do you want me to love or encourage today, and how?"

Often with preschoolers even making a craft or a card to be given to a parent or a neighbor begins the early thought of encouraging someone else. Likewise, preschool leaders can ask the Lord how he wants them to encourage each child each morning and that Spirit of encouragement and expressing love will multiply in the children. Be creative in thinking up other ways in which you might weave in this experience.

Make an Oikos Map with your kids and put it on the fridge. Practice the Include Me Prayer. Can you think of some other easy ways?

Imagine what it might look like for a person to grow up in a ministry environment like this. I've seen it, and it's amazing.

SMALL GROUPS

During the Core time, we might begin by going around the circle giving each person a chance to share briefly about a need or concern in their life.

We then do a Discovery Bible Study on a passage that speaks to God's sufficiency or provision. For example, Colossians 1:9-10:

> I pray that God will fill you with the knowledge of his will with all the wisdom and understanding that his Spirit gives you so that you might live a life worthy of him, fully pleasing in his sight, bearing fruit in every good work, and increasing grace in the knowledge of God.

After the DBS, we'll give each person a brief opportunity to share the biggest struggle or stress they're currently facing. Once someone shares, the group will pause, making space for God to help us See-Feel-Respond. After that moment of reflection, we'll pray for the person, offer encouragement, or provide practical support as needed.

DISCIPLESHIP GROUPS

We follow the Lifegroup approach above, doing a DBS in our Learn It time followed by encouraging/praying for one another in our Live It time.

STAFF MEETING

I'm sure you can see how you might include this in a staff experience. Most often we do it in small groups, but it's also powerful to pick one person and have the whole team listen to the Lord for loving and encouraging them.

#4 Weaving in Talking with Others About the Lord

Weaving this experience into the Circles is a bit different than the other experiences because the whole point is to join Jesus in having spiritual conversations with people who often are not yet believers.

As a result, when we weave this thread into the various circles of the church, we are generally training or practicing the Starting Points together. Here are some examples:

MAIN WORSHIP GATHERINGS

A simple way to weave this thread into this context is to invite a moment of reflection/listening at the end of the service, asking the Lord to bring to mind someone in our sphere of influence who needs to know the Good news.

We might commit to focusing on this person as we engage in Prayer-Care-Share in the coming week. We pray for the person every day. We look for practical ways to express our genuine care for them. We make time for any conversation they might want to initiate or that the Lord might orchestrate.

The Include Me Prayer is another simple way to exhort people to give Jesus room to create an opportunity for them to talk with others about him. Ask people to email or text with any story of how God included them. Consider sharing those on Sunday with the permission of the person who shared them.

156

One of my favorites is to use a whiteboard on Sunday to draw the Bridge Illustration. We, of course, equip our people with a 4x6 card and a pencil so that after I've taught it, we can draw it together. Then, I challenge them to find one person during the week to ask this question:

> My church is teaching everyone how to draw a picture that summarizes the whole Bible in three minutes. I'm supposed to practice it. Could I show it to you and you give me feedback?

Be creative! That's the fun of weaving disciple making into the fabric of your church. Don't forget that sharing stories is a great way to "show" people what discipleship looks like in every day life. Jesus loves to let us be creative as we weave with him.

CHILDREN'S MINISTRY AND THE FAMILY

There are lots of fun and creative ways to include children in learning to Talk with Others about the Lord. Here are a few:

- Have a missionary or someone who recently returned from an outreach come and share creatively about the people and place where they took the love of Jesus. Use pictures, sounds, food, activities, or anything else that helps connect the children to the people of that area. Share stories of what Jesus did. The Holy Spirit will use all of these efforts to stir up a love for the nations of the world inside the children.
- When you're with your own kids, practice Prayer-Care-Share. Show them what it looks like to love and share with people in your oikos.
- For older kids, you might give them a silicone bracelet that has symbols that tell the Gospel story. Encourage them to wear it and equip them to explain it.

- At our church, we are committed to the Kairos Prison Ministry[51] and each time our teams enter a prison for the weekend encounter retreat, they carry with them pictures and cards our younger children have made for those who are incarcerated. After the retreat, we share with the kids how meaningful their contribution was to those who received it.

STUDENT MINISTRY AND SMALL GROUPS

Here are some ways to include this experience in these circles:

- Practicing drawing the Bridge Illustration.[52]
- Drawing an Oikos Map and praying together for the lost in our individual spheres of influence.
- Practicing sharing a 15-second testimony.
- Doing a DBS on a passage that expresses God's heart to reconcile the world.
- Going to a park or other public place and offering to pray for people using The Miracle Question and giving Jesus room to create a spiritual conversation.

DISCIPLESHIP GROUPS

All the same ways described above work in this circle. That being said, this circle is perhaps the best one for actually going together to talk with others about the Lord.

This ministry context provides a unique environment that none of the other circles can touch. In it, you have the accountability and the personal connection to help people bravely go where they might not be willing to go alone.

---

51 "Kairos Prison Ministry International | Bringing Hope and Healing to Incarcerated Individuals," Accessed September 4, 2024. https://kairosprisonministry.org/.
52 See DiscipleMakingThreads.com.

If discipleship only consists of sitting in a coffee shop and having a Bible study, then it will never reproduce and likely won't reach very many people with the Gospel. Worse, it robs people of answering the Kingdom Calling that Jesus has issued. Don't forget, this is all a part of enjoying and following him. Don't keep it from those you disciple.

THE BROADER IMPACT

I was part of a wonderful church once that often celebrated how much money we gave to the denominational missions agency. The church was a generous generator of funds for *others* to do missions, but the people of this church weren't being personally mobilized.

As threads of reproducible disciple making are woven into the fabric of your church, all of this changes. Stories of Jesus's power and courage of humble people following him will become normal and invigorating.

These simple Starting Points not only help a person begin to live their life as an adventurer with Jesus, but as the Starting Points become part of the fabric of your church, you'll find your outreaches much more well attended. Your training for international outreaches changes too because now the people have already been equipped or at least familiarized with Starting Points for how to have spiritual conversations with others.

When these threads are combined with a strategy to reach the nations, you'll be surprised by who answers the Lord's call to take the Gospel to the ends of the earth.

CHAPTER 20

THE ROLE OF THE
LEAD WEAVERS

Weaving in threads of disciple making is a focused, persistent approach to church ministry. Like many lead pastors, the tedium of disciple making initially frustrated my "Get'r done" nature. I wanted to see change fast…I wanted to be able to measure it…I wanted to create a team, pick a leader, and give them whatever they needed to get'r done. But now I'm convinced that's not Jesus' way.

Weaving in threads of disciple making is a focused, persistent approach to church ministry.

Make no mistake, there's a place for the charging, visionary leader. Absolutely. But when the goal is to create a disciple making culture in the prevailing American Church model, the role of the visionary leader isn't to keep exhorting people, "Faster! We need to step it up! Let's get'r done!"

The majority of people—like 93%—don't receive this kind of exhortation as healthy encouragement.[53] They receive it as pressure. They hear it as "You're not doing good enough." That's not

---

53 Kubicek, Jeremie and Cockram, Steve (2016). *The 5 Voices: How to Communicate Effectively with Everyone You Lead.* Hoboken, NJ: Wiley.

encouragement, that's a beat down and it leads to people having a general sense of being unappreciated. Fortunately, there's a better use of the strengths of the visionary leader.

THE SMOKE OF THE BATTLEFIELD

The most respected generals are the ones who lead their troops into battle. There's something incredibly genuine and compelling about a leader who smells like the smoke of the battlefield.

A much more valuable role for the visionary, apostolic leader is to use his voice to shout, "We're going the right way! Don't give up! I'm with you! I'm proud of you!"

In the battle for creating a disciple making culture in a church, the leader(s) actually need to be making disciples themselves. Disciple making isn't a program a leader can delegate. When a leader is personally engaged in a Lifegroup or leading a D-group you can tell. Their instructions and questions; their encouragement and strategy, all carry the aroma of one who is actually in the fight. A leader who is in the fight is one of the most important agents for creating a disciple making culture. Why? Because this is how Jesus led.

PASTORING IN THE DIGITAL AGE

We're already in an age where any person on the planet can access the content of the best teachers on the planet through any number of digital platforms. Not a week goes by that someone in our church doesn't mention to me some wonderful teaching they heard on a podcast or video platform. This will only be enhanced through advancing technology.

Almost any person on the planet can access the content of the best teachers on the planet.

This is the one thing that all of the best teachers combined cannot do for our church.

How am I supposed to compete with all of this incredible teaching content? There's no way I can…and I'm not supposed to. The reality is that I have a much more important responsibility: To cultivate a disciple making culture. This is the one thing that all of the best teachers combined cannot do for our church. It can only be led by those who are actually in the local church.

Previously, when I was wrestling with my addiction to Sunday morning, I thought my top priority was preaching on Sunday (our church thought that too). While it's true I must ensure we have quality teaching on Sunday, I have the role of Chief Culture Creator. I'm determined that we will become a church that shows people how to enjoy and follow Jesus together in a way that they can show others how to enjoy and follow him too.

THE PRIORITY OF PRAYER

Another key role of the lead weaver is that of intercession. For the present, understand intercession as praying prayers for others that they ought to be praying for themselves but either can't or won't.

A disciple making culture won't materialize just by organizing, mobilizing, and counting. It comes about when leaders persist in prayer for it and don't stop.

In prayer, you're not just placing your requests upon God's heavenly doorstep, you're acknowledging your great need for Jesus. This is, in fact, an amazingly counterintuitive part of how God makes straight your path. Remember Proverbs 3:5-6?...*Trust in the Lord with all your heart and lean not on your own understanding. In all your ways* **acknowledge him,** *and he will make your path straight.*

Persistent intercession humbles us because prayer puts us in the presence of Jesus. His presence always produces humility in those who love him. Even before a word has left your mouth, your acknowledgment of his lordship, wisdom, strategy, and sufficiency gives him room to bless.

The people you lead will never know of your labor in prayer, but they will experience the fruit of it.

CHAPTER 21

AN INVITATION

If you've read this short book and felt something stirring in you to weave threads of disciple making into the fabric of your church, I have one more encouragement for you: Don't try it alone.

Creating a disciple making culture requires changing your existing culture while at the same time leading your church, a process akin to the old illustration of trying to change the propeller on your airplane without losing altitude.

It's far easier to do this when you have a cohort of other pastors/ leaders going after the same goal in their church too. So here's the invitation…Come take a walk with me and some other like-minded leaders who are determined to break their addiction to Sunday morning and create a disciple making culture in their churches.

At the time of writing *Threads*, this "walk" consists of eight Zoom calls during which we practice the Core Experiences together, and then, before our next week's call, we pick one experience and weave it into one of the Circles/contexts of our church. In our following call, we share how things went and what we've learned.

Working with pastors and members of their staff team, I've seen this cohort and other training experiences have an accelerating effect on the transformation of their church culture to one of disciple making.

Remember, we always train harder and better when we train with a team. That's the invitation I'm extending to you.

For information about what cohort and training experiences might be currently available, email Info@DisciplemakingThreads.com.

A SUMMARY OF STARTING POINTS

It bears repeating: Starting Points are simply that, places to start. Don't make them rules. They are valuable only to the degree that they help a person begin to enjoy and follow Jesus.

That having been said, the Starting Points are important because otherwise the person you disciple will struggle with how to disciple someone else.

The Starting Points are rooted in God's unchanging Word. Here are just some of the Scriptures which comprise the biblical basis for each one:

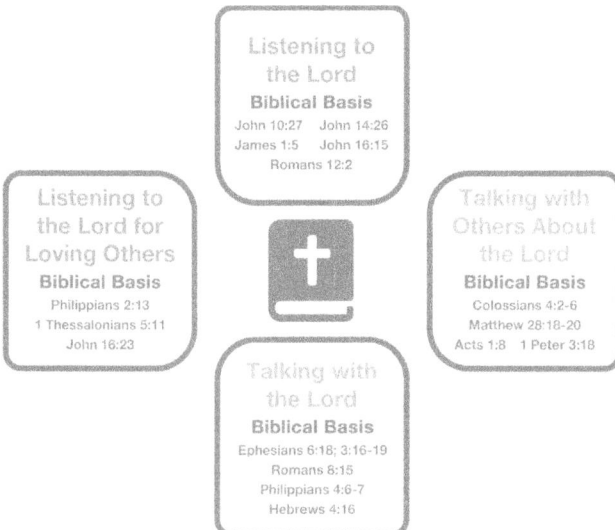

Listening to the Lord
Biblical Basis
John 10:27   John 14:26
James 1:5   John 16:15
Romans 12:2

Listening to the Lord for Loving Others
Biblical Basis
Philippians 2:13
1 Thessalonians 5:11
John 16:23

Talking with Others About the Lord
Biblical Basis
Colossians 4:2-6
Matthew 28:18-20
Acts 1:8   1 Peter 3:18

Talking with the Lord
Biblical Basis
Ephesians 6:18; 3:16-19
Romans 8:15
Philippians 4:6-7
Hebrews 4:16

Listening to the Lord

DISCOVERY BIBLE STUDY

A simple inductive study that is the Starting Point for disciple making in the House to House circle or in the circle of Life on Life Discipleship. Though there are different iterations of a DBS, the way we utilize it is like this:

- The passage of Scripture is read twice in different translations.
- The group studies the passage together asking these two questions: 1) What does this passage reveal that's true about God and his character, priorities, or ways? 2) What does it reveal about people, their character, priorities, or ways?
- Then we answer, How is this good news to me?
- We follow this up by practicing one of the Core Experiences.

I WANT YOU TO KNOW...

A prompt to give people as a Starting Point for learning to Listen to the Lord. Utilize this after a DBS or sermon, giving people 1-2 minutes to let Jesus complete this sentence. Remind them that the Holy Spirit always speaks consistent with Scripture, consistent with God's character as a Good Father, and always in a positive tone, not a condemning tone— even when convicting us of sin.

Using a journal is a great discipline and helps people keep a record of their spiritual journey.

I WILL...

A person uses the "I will" statement to personally reflect in partnership with the Holy Spirit to determine what their obedience step should be in light of what they've heard.

Talking with the Lord

DISCOVERY PRAYER

Discovery Prayer uses Scripture as the fuel for engaging prayer using the pattern of Thank-Declare-Ask.

We begin by looking at what the passage reveals about God for which we can **thank** him. As someone prays, others should listen. The Holy Spirit loves when we pray together and will often bring a related thought to mind or a picture that helps us thank God more specifically or personally.

We can also look at the passage for what it says is true about us or others. We can **declare** these things in prayer, exercising our spiritual authority in Christ.

Finally, we **ask** for more of what the passage is telling us Jesus has for us.

As we pray, it's helpful to pray shorter prayers and then pause, listening to Jesus, allowing him to direct or expand our prayers.

Listening to the Lord for Loving Others

SEE-FEEL-RESPOND

Use this approach to get God's perspective and insight for strengthening, comforting, and encouraging others. Ask the Lord what he **sees**, what he **feels**, and how he wants you to **respond**. He may give you something to pray, a picture to share, an act of service to render, or simple words of encouragement to build up someone.

Talking with Others About the Lord

PRAYER-CARE-SHARE

A Starting Point that levels the playing field so that everyone—regardless of their personality or experience—can begin to live life on mission. Refer to Chapter 10 for a more detailed explanation of this Starting Point.

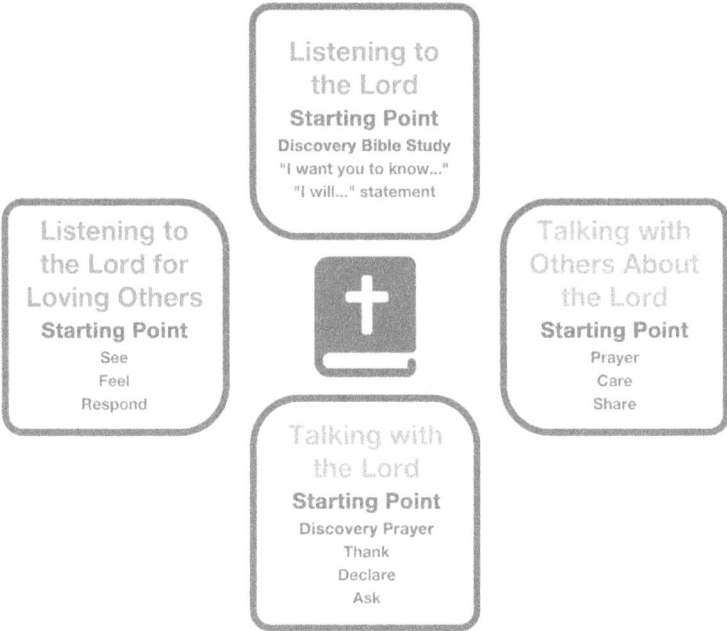

Listening to
the Lord
Starting Point
Discovery Bible Study
"I want you to know..."
"I will..." statement

Listening to
the Lord for
Loving Others
Starting Point
See
Feel
Respond

Talking with
Others About
the Lord
Starting Point
Prayer
Care
Share

Talking with
the Lord
Starting Point
Discovery Prayer
Thank
Declare
Ask

OTHER HELPFUL DEFINITIONS

15-SECOND TESTIMONY

A brief, personal story of how Jesus made a difference in your life. This isn't your "salvation story," this is generally more relevant to the need expressed by a person for whom you've just prayed. It can be easily begun with the phrase: *There was a time in my life…* Refer to page 91 to see an example I provided of my experience with JoJo.

BRIDGE ILLUSTRATION

A simple drawing that expresses how much God loves us. It takes practice to draw, talk, and relate to the other person all at the same time, but it's a Starting Point every follower of Jesus should master. For a video that walks you through a short presentation of The Bridge Illustration, visit DiscipleMakingThreads.com.

INCLUDE ME PRAYER

A simple prayer to pray wherever you are, whomever you're with: *Jesus, would you include me in what you're doing?*

Jesus isn't looking to *use* you. Like a good father, he wants to *include* you. There's something fun, adventurous, and personal about this perspective.

Though the Include Me Prayer is part of Prayer-Care-Share, it's such a powerful standalone Starting Point. Remember its impact on Leo. Start praying it and see Jesus show up!

LISTENING TO THE LORD FOR FREEDOM

For support everyone can employ to receive freedom from sin, ungodly beliefs, and wounds, visit DiscipleMakingThreads.com/StartingPoints.

For in-depth training and resources, I encourage you to go to FreedomPrayer.org.

MIRACLE QUESTION

A simple question to ask that gives room for a spiritual conversation. *If God could do a miracle in your life, what would it be, and could I pray for it?*

OIKOS MAP

A drawing of our personal sphere of influence which helps us identify special people for whom we can pray (see page 93).

MORE ON LISTENING TO THE LORD

If the idea of Listening to the Lord sounds more threatening than thrilling, and you're more resistant than reassured, perhaps this story will help.

Recently, a pastor-friend of mine met with me for coffee. His church tradition has a very strong emphasis on the Word, but less strong on the Spirit. He'd heard me share about my having met Leo and was intrigued by my emphasis on both the Word and the Spirit, specifically the idea of Listening to the Lord.

We got our coffee, engaged in small talk for a bit, but then, he lowered his voice and leaned in as if we might be overheard talking about something subversive, and he asked me, "Kirk, I'm intrigued by the idea of Listening to the Lord but I have to ask,...'Is it safe? I mean, what about the sufficiency of Scripture?'"

Good shepherds should always ask questions like these.

I love that he was asking these questions (maybe you are asking them too). His questions showed his genuine concern for shepherding people well.

Good shepherds should always ask questions like these.

As I stated in Chapter 7, I believe in the sufficiency of Scripture. The Bible is God's unchanging Truth for all people for all time, sufficient for salvation and a life that glorifies God. The doctrine of the sufficiency of Scripture is vitally important, and it's the only reason why I believe the Holy Spirit speaks in a spiritual voice that all believers can discern and count on. Had God not told us in Scripture that we could personally interact with the Spirit of Jesus—listening and talking with him— humankind would never have imagined that we could. Consider the major, human-created religions: None of them promises or encourages our having a personal relationship with God. Only when the One, True God reveals himself in his Word do we see that he desires to know us and for us to know him.[54]

Through the incarnation and all that Jesus accomplished, God, himself, is inviting us into a relationship so personal that he describes it as Parent/child and Groom/bride.[55] These human relationships are based on communication, which is part of the reason God provides them as our point of reference for understanding how we are to relate to him. These relationships are intimate above all others and yet, they only point to the ultimate intimacy that we are to have with the risen Christ who Scripture says actually lives within us.[56] What groom ignores his bride? What good father refuses to affirm each of his children personally?

I decided that if I truly believe in the sufficiency of Scripture, then I must believe and embrace what Scripture is telling me about the kind of intimate interaction I can have with God. I don't want to let church

---

54 Genesis 1:28; 3:8-9; 12:1-17:27; Micah 6:8; John 14:17; Revelation 21:1-5…and many, many more places in Scripture.
55 1 John 3:1; Revelation 19:7-9 among others.
56 Galatians 2:20; Ephesians 3:14

tradition trump the Bible, leading me to quench the Holy Spirit. Nor do I want to let fear rob our people of the joy and power of an actual personal relationship with Jesus. Rather, I want to courageously and expectantly receive all that the Bible tells us Jesus won for us through his death and resurrection.

If I truly believe in the sufficiency of Scripture, then I must believe and embrace what Scripture is telling me about the kind of intimate interaction I can have with God.

My friend also asked, "Is it safe?" Remember the three-posted pasture I described in Chapter 7: the Word of God, Spirit of God, and People of God? It actually works as an effective safeguard in local church life.

I've found that when we stay within the pasture, people actually learn to experience Jesus personally. Even when a person "hears" incorrectly, their ongoing involvement in the community of the People of God allows for quick, gentle correction. People are already carrying around non-biblical beliefs in their heads; by teaching them to Listen to the Lord within the three-posted pasture, we are actually providing an opportunity for these errant beliefs to be exposed so we may bring them into alignment with God's better way. For people living within the three-posted pasture—from not-yet-believers to spiritual mothers and fathers—big heretical catastrophes almost never happen. On the contrary, the pasture provides the God-ordained way for sound doctrine to prevail.[57]

---

57 My one caveat regards mental health. Very rarely, I've experienced a challenge in this area with a person wrestling with an issue of mental health.

This has always been God's way. Don't forget to whom the Epistles were written: normal every day followers of Jesus. None had advanced degrees in theology. They, like us, were dependent upon the Word of God, the Spirit of God, and the People of God. This is Christianity 101.

In Chapter 7, I describe how I use the "I want you to know…" statement as a Starting Point for Listening to the Lord. I had done this exercise with small groups, but not with our entire congregation and was a bit anxious. I wondered, "Is it presumptuous of us to expect God to speak on demand?" This is a different question than the one asking does God speak. I was wondering, "Does God speak when we want him to?"

I find that he usually does. Don't I speak to my wife when she wants to talk? Doesn't a dad speak to his child, especially when the child is eager to listen to his father's wisdom? The Bible repeatedly instructs us to filter our understanding and expectations of God through the lens of these relationships.

When we engage the Word of God in our Sunday gatherings (or elsewhere) and then take time to give the Spirit of God room to impress his thoughts upon us, he is just as eager to meet us as he was when he walked in the Garden in the cool of the evening to be with Adam and Eve—he's still that same God.

WHAT DOES GOD SAY?

A more important question has to do with our expectation, "What does the Lord say? Does God say what we want him to say or answer questions like Aladdin's genie?"

Look at that question through the Father/child goggles. Does a good father relate to his children that way? Sometimes a child desperately wants to know or to have something and their parent chooses to withhold it or give them something different.

Remember what Jesus said about the Holy Spirit? He will teach you and remind you of everything I've said to you. Paul told us the Holy Spirit will create a desire in us for God's will and the power to follow it.[58]

> **We were designed by God to relate to him as a Father— the Best of Fathers. He actually wants us to treat him like one.**

God wants us to bring our pressing questions and concerns to him.[59] When we do, he often does what good fathers always do when their children are distressed: He comforts them. He reminds them of his love. He pulls them close so they feel the safety of his presence. Sometimes a good father will impart a solution or answer to a direct problem, sometimes he won't, but he always comforts, strengthens, and encourages.

Inherently, we all know this to be true. Why? Because we were designed by God to relate to him as a Father—the Best of Fathers. He actually wants us to treat him like one.

Don't forget about how sin, lies, and wounds can impact our connection to God. Chapter 11 reminds us of the simple, yet powerful

---

58 John 14:26, Philippians 2:13
59 Ephesians 6:13; 1 Peter 5:7; Matthew 6:9-13 and others.

weapons at our disposal to remove these obstructions from our experience of God.

WHERE TO SAFELY START

The best way I know to safely practice Listening to the Lord is to personally do it. Start with reading and meditating on the Word of God, then with your journal use the "I want you to know..." Starting Point. I believe you'll sense Jesus bringing thoughts to your mind that encourage you and affirm his love for you. Perhaps it will be directly related to what you read in Scripture or just something that aligns with Scripture. Use the four ways in Chapter 7 to test and approve what you hear and, if you're uncertain about what you received, then run it by other trusted followers of Jesus (the People of God).

Try Listening to the Lord within the context of your personal D-group or some other context. Jesus will show up. (This is what I did with Leo, remember?) If someone in the group shares something that you know isn't biblical, don't just correct them by telling them, show them where in the Bible God reveals what's actually true. The vast majority of the time the level of "heresy" is very low and commonly involves a works-based righteousness issue or something related to shame/condemnation. These are easy to correct, and when they are, you'll feel the joy of a groomsman/bridesmaid getting to see the Groom drawing his bride closer to himself.

Ready for a
next step?

Having worked with over 300 churches, Kirk has learned that intentionality and persistence over time are the keys to changing the culture of a church.

If you're a lead pastor and ready to begin the journey of creating a disciple making culture in your church, don't go it alone. Let the Threads Coaching Team help you and your staff.

ABOUT THE AUTHOR
Kirk Freeman

Kirk Freeman isn't an expert at reproducible disciple making, but he's unswervingly committed to it. He's also committed to helping pastors who are looking to weave disciple making into the fabric of their church. After pursuing a career as a country music songwriter, he realized he wasn't as good as his mother said he was. He spent a decade in the Christian publishing industry in Nashville and Dallas, before graduating from seminary and joining a church staff team first as their Worship Pastor and then as Executive Pastor. In 2002 he and his family moved to San Antonio to plant CrossBridge Community Church where he has been lead pastor for over 20 years.

He and his wife, Debbie, met in elementary school and now have a growing family of wonderful daughters and sons-in-law.

FOR SPEAKING OR TRAINING INQUIRIES, email info@DiscipleMakingThreads.com.

CONNECT: Instagram.com/KirkFreeman_